Stan is an excellent speaker, coach, and friend. He is a true inspiration and provides guidance based on his own real-life experiences. Our staff and management team have benefited from his counseling and we look forward to continuing our collaboration with Stan for many years to come.

Hash Hashemian
President & CEO
AMS Corporation

Life's journey can be embraced or challenged and I was so lucky three decades ago when Stan came into my life, assumed my leadership role of a huge portfolio and team and made me feel free to relocate from Texas to California. Leadership today is defined by syncing your soul with decisions, challenges and opportunities going forward with your IQ and previous experience. I call this soulful leadership and Stan came into my world path and taught me all about that in relationships at work and home, humor even when you are in a tough situation and his positive and loving outlook at life and everyone around him.

John Combs
Principal
River Rock Real Estate Group

The timing that Stan and I met could not have been better. A foundational mentor and friend, his guidance has been pivotal in my transition and growth from the field to the business world. His leadership and coaching have improved my focus, growth and prioritization.

Fred Wakefield MBA
Growth and Development Specialist
Retired NFL Athlete (8 years)

Living a
RICH
— and —
INTENTIONAL LIFE

Stan Gibson

Copyright © 2020 by Stan Gibson

All rights reserved. No part of this book may be reproduced or transmitted in any form or by any means, electronic or mechanical, including photocopying, recording or by any information storage and retrieval system without permission in writing from the publisher.

OxygenPlus Publishing
Placida, Florida 33946
sgibson@oxygen-plus.net

Printed in the United States of America

Cover Design by Kadi Schultz
Chapter Head Design by William Love
Book Design by WORDART, LLC West Des Moines, IA

TABLE OF CONTENTS

Introduction
LIVING WITH CLARITY
CHAPTER 1 Life Becomes Rich When Death Becomes Certain 1
CHAPTER 2 Getting Your Priorities Straight 11
CHAPTER 3 Know Who You Are... and Who You're NOT 19

MANAGING ENERGY... IT'S MORE SCIENCE THAN I THOUGHT
CHAPTER 4 A Reason for Waking Up 39
CHAPTER 5 The Physical Side of Life.. 51
CHAPTER 6 Relationships... a Matter of Life and Death 79
CHAPTER 7 The Zen Side of Life 89

LIVING WITH INTENTION
CHAPTER 8 Simplifying our Stuff and our Experiences................... 109
CHAPTER 9 It's Easier to Get a Good Brand than It Is to Lose a Bad One... 121
CHAPTER 10 I'll Take a Good Routine Over Discipline Any Day! 129

CONCLUSION
The Obstacle is The Way...The Hardest Chapter to Write 143

Afterword
Acknowledgements
About the Author

INTRODUCTION

MY STORY... AND MY DESIRE TO CHANGE YOUR STORY!

Welcome to *Living a Rich and Intentional Life*! I've been giving my message as a keynote speaker around the country for several years now. About a week after a speaking engagement in Orlando last year, I received the greatest message a speaker can receive when a young lady wrote, "I never thought my life could be changed in 60 minutes! My husband and I are on a new path feeling energy like we've never felt before." And then the kicker question came, "Where do I buy your book? I need to send it to my family and friends."

Well, that was going to be a problem... mostly because I'd never intended to become an author. But, over the course of years, I've witnessed so many leaders begging to get "unstuck" in life. Today's leaders are clamoring for more energy, purpose, and zest for life. In the words of my dad, "Sometimes we're damn sick and tired of being damn sick and tired." I see it... I hear it... and I've lived it!

Now I've put together a collection of stories, research, and, hopefully, a bit of humor to deliver a message that encourages everyone to live a rich and intentional life! It's truly possible... it really is! Just stick with me throughout this book as we explore your purpose, energy, and quest for intentional living.

My research began 15 years ago when I was on vacation and, uncharacteristically, I decided to start and finish a book within the week. While I LOVE to read, finishing books in short order is not in my DNA, nor is finding one that I can't put down. However, I heard a great quote that has carried me past that guilt: "Read as many books as you can; if it doesn't interest you, then file it away. But if you find a book you really love, READ IT TWICE."

For me, that book was *The Power of Full Engagement* by Jim Loehr and Tony Schwartz. That book captivated me and taught me everything I now believe and passionately use to coach leaders. Using their innovative approach to managing and harnessing energy, Loehr and Schwartz were on the cutting edge of transferring the tools and rituals they used to train world class athletes and infusing these same paradigms into the business world.

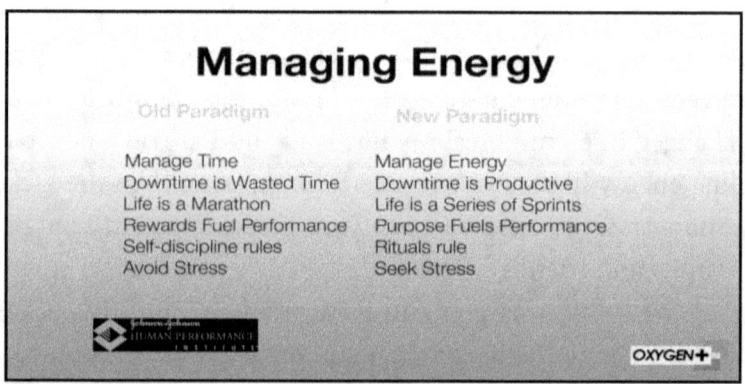

This was the first leadership book that taught me the paradigm that "leaders take care of themselves first and foremost!" Leadership is less about life balance and time management. Instead, ENERGY is now the new mantra. Sprinting vs. long distance, rest and recovery, rituals and seeking stress, and having purpose over rewards made so much more sense. These shifts in lifestyle sent me and countless other coaches, leaders, and self-help gurus down a new path that is consistent with most modern-day leadership and personal development mantras.

In this book, I will specifically talk about the physiological effects of managing energy through our purpose and physical, emotional, and mental energies. ALL four must be within an acceptable range for you to feel and be totally energized.

I strongly believe that if you aren't doing well on the home front, you're not effective at work. On the other hand, if you aren't hitting on all cylinders at work, you won't be all that pleasant to be around at home. This book is a collection of tips and tricks that can be read in chapters from start to finish or sections that interest you most. It's years of research and more importantly personal trial and error as both mentor and mentee. Most importantly, it's meant to challenge everyone, no matter the season of life you're travelling through. Whether you're a young Gen Z looking for wisdom or a crafty Baby Boomer looking to leave a legacy, this book has something for everyone. So read away... get intentional and let me show you why being selfish is a good thing!

> *"For I know the plans I have for you,"* declares the Lord,
> *"plans to prosper you and not harm you, plans*
> *to give you hope and a future."*
> Jeremiah 29:11

dailystoic

"If you are careless and lazy now and keep putting things off and always deferring the day after which you will attend to yourself, you will not notice that you are making no progress but you will live and die as someone quite ordinary."

EPICTETUS

LIVING WITH CLARITY

CHAPTER 1

LIFE BECOMES RICH WHEN DEATH BECOMES CERTAIN

Although my passion for living a rich and intentional life started over 15 years ago, my journey officially started unexpecedly nine years ago while having a simple dinner with my wife, Sharon. We've always enjoyed going out together and, although we've known each other since third grade... YES, 3rd grade, we never run out of things to talk about and truly love our time together.

On this particular night, we had just sat down to order our meal and saw a friend that we hadn't seen in a few years. Our friend, Jerry, and his wife were some of the first friends we met when we moved to Des Moines in the early 90s. We took a few weekend vacations together and shared great laughs and a lifetime bond.

Jerry and his wife are no ordinary people. Jerry is one of those friends that you admire on so many levels. Jerry started a very successful financial firm many years ago and is a magnificent CEO and leader. In addition, Jerry has a great wife and wonderful kids and an extended family, as he and his wife served as foster parents.

And moreover, Jerry and his wife, Nancy, have a successful marriage ministry and have traveled the world helping couples reset their marriages with Christian principles. Additionally, Jerry is an author who wrote a great book titled *LifeFocus... Achieving a Life of Purpose and Influence*.

So, you get the drift. Jerry and his wife are solid and, although we hadn't seen them in a few years, he's someone my wife and I will always marvel at because of his accomplishments, humility, and growth along the way. After we ordered our meal, we spotted Jerry, and we spent maybe five minutes at most catching up on what he and Nancy had been up to, as well as their children. We said our good byes, and Jerry quietly walked away.

About five minutes passed, and Jerry walked back over. He looked at my wife and me and said, "You know, after I walked away, I thought that I should come back over and tell you... I have cancer, and I have a 50/50 shot at living five years."

Mic drop...
Jaw drop...
I was stunned to say the least.

This stuff doesn't happen to people like Jerry, especially not when he's in his early 50s and had told me a few years earlier that he developed a life plan for the next 50 years (yes, living past 100) because he knew he could accomplish so much more in the second half of his life.

Well, in times like this, one never knows what to say. To say that we were speechless is an understatement. The only thing I could muster out of my mouth was a weak and sympathetic, "Jerry, I'm so sorry... I don't know what to say."

In typical Jerry fashion, he said, "OH, NO! I didn't come

over here to make you feel sorry for me. You see, although I wish I didn't have this diagnosis, it's literally one of the best things that ever happened. I'm finally saying NO to *the wrong things* so I can say YES to *the right things*. I'm having the most intimate conversations with my wife I ever imagined. Shortly after being diagnosed and going through surgery, I took my family on a vacation and asked them, 'If I'm not here in three years, what do you need from me between now and then?' "

Over the next 60 days, he spent time with each member of his family, individually, to have what had to have been the most intimate conversations he's ever had as a husband and father.

As Jerry finished his conversation with Sharon and me, he looked at us with an engaging look that only Jerry could do. He leaned in and said the most fantastic thing that I had ever heard:

"Life becomes rich when death becomes certain."

I don't know why, but that phrase was new to me and couldn't have been more profound. It has stuck with me ever since and has become a key theme when I speak at events around the country. From that point on, I've asked every audience member to whom I've spoken, "Why do we wait for life to deal us a crap sandwich and then decide to get serious about living?" We all believe we are invincible. It doesn't matter what season of life we're in, life tragedies always happen to someone else... right?

Now for the good news. That meeting was nine years ago, and I met up with Jerry last year to give him insight about the speeches I've given around the country and to thank him for letting me see life differently. Jerry is the picture of health, and God is probably letting Jerry work on his plan to live another 50 years. After Jerry looked at the slides used in my speeches, he said, "Stan, everything your message embodies is exactly what's keeping me alive."

Anxiety and stress are keys to weakening the immune system, causing disease and life altering diagnoses. Now, my wife and I are extremely focused on our physical, emotional, mental, and spiritual being and the routines to execute them flawlessly. Jerry and Nancy live with extreme intention, and he's throttled back his work life to gain more quality time with family, grandchildren, and friends. He still works, but he has delegated a lot of his CEO responsibilities to the next level of leaders in his organization.

Most of all, he's living a rich life!

My wife and I had a chance to go to dinner with Jerry and Nancy a few months ago. We had plenty to talk about, especially if you hang around to the final chapters of this book (no peeking ahead please). We had a wonderful night and reminisced about the trips we took when we were younger and how blessed we are that our children all lead wonderful lives.

As the evening was winding down, I pondered a bit and then had the urge to ask Jerry, "So just what are you doing these days that you're most proud of?"

He looked at us and said, "You know, after my surgery, my wife suggested I get a hobby. Being Type A and needing to enjoy life more, a friend suggested we take a painting class, which is something I had never considered. So every Wednesday afternoon, five or six of us meet in an art studio in the instructor's basement. We have a glass of wine and learn the art of painting."

"Really?" I asked. "Do you have anything you've finished or anything I can see?" Well, that was an invitation for Jerry to pull out his phone and show me his newest creations.

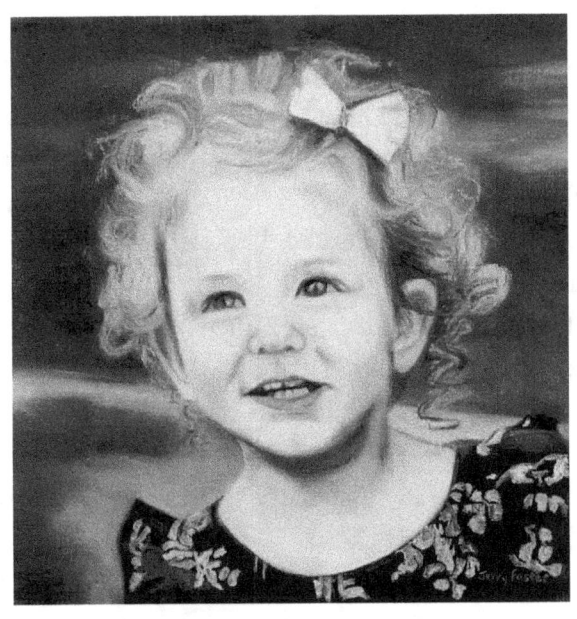

Yeah... kind of cool, huh? And these are just two of the many pictures he showed me. The little girl is one of his granddaughters, and the other picture is of Jerry's dad, brother, and grandson titled, *My Father's Legacy*. And just like nine years ago, my jaw is still dropping!

As I looked at Jerry, I asked, "How did you paint these wonderful paintings?"

At that time, his wife Nancy leaned in and said, "This is what getting a cancer diagnosis will do to you."

This is Jerry leading a rich and intentional life!

We all love a good "Jerry story." We love to think about what life would look like if we had no fear and only a few years to live. We think and contemplate often what living a rich life really means. For many, we're so busy living life that we don't have the time or the ability to risk our job or the lifestyle we've come accustomed to. And for many of you reading this book, it feels like the more responsibilities we take after entering the workforce, getting married, having children, accumulating mortgages and additional responsibility, the more elusive it becomes to live a carefree and intentional life.

I won't feed you the belief that you have to throw everything away and begin living your passion. Life is far more complicated than that. However, this book is about small changes regardless of what season of life you're in. It's about lifestyle changes over time giving you more energy to make the right decisions. And while millennials and those of us a little older believe we've cornered the market of living in a pressure cooker, I'm finding it's our youth that's reaching out asking questions and seeking a life truly worth living.

We live in a digitally obese world where children and young adults are reaching epidemic portions of anxiety, synthetic relationships, and depression (also called digital dementia). To that point, do you know what the most requested class at Yale University is? (Yes, Yale, the third-oldest institution of higher education in the US, which produced such famous alums as George H.W. Bush, Paul Newman, John Kerry, Jodi Foster, and Oliver Stone, just to name a few.) The most sought after course, which was only introduced in January 2018 is… HAPPINESS 101 (now titled: Psych 157: Psychology and the Good Life). This amazing class started with just 300 students signed up. Within three days, another 300 students signed up. Within three more days, the class totaled more than 1,200 students, which is one-fourth of Yale's undergraduates. The course is taught by psychology professor Laurie Santos, who teaches students how to lead happier, more satisfying lives via twice-weekly lectures.

Dr. Santos speculated that Yale students are interested in the class because in high school they had to de-prioritize their happiness to gain admission to the school and adopted harmful life habits that led to what she called "the mental health crises we're seeing at places like Yale." A 2013 report by the Yale College Council found that *more than half* of undergraduates sought mental health care from the university during their time there.

She hopes that by taking the course among friends, students will experience less anxiety than they do in other courses, and she encourages all students to enroll in the course on a pass/fail basis, which illustrates her argument that the achievement-based things Yale undergrads associate with life satisfaction don't actually increase happiness.

"Scientists didn't realize this in the same way ten or so years ago, that our institutions about what will make us happy, like winning the lottery and getting a good grade are totally wrong," Dr.

Santos said. The class has now evolved into a free, online, 10-week class taught by Dr. Santos, called "*The Science of Well-Being*," and when the learning platform, Coursera, started offering it online for free, a whopping 255,000 people signed up.

Basic themes of the class are covered as well throughout this book, including simple practices such as "buying experiences, not things," practicing gratitude, knowing who you are... and who you're not, and how they're all deeply tied to happiness.

So let's continue to dive in to explore purpose, living with intention, creating abundant energy, and self-awareness.

Chapter 1 Key Concepts

- ☒ When death becomes certain... life becomes rich.

- ☒ Learn to say "no" to the wrong things so you can say "Yes" to the right things.

- ☒ Anxiety and stress are key causes of breaking down the immune system and causing disease and sickness.

- ☒ No matter what season of life we're in, we're all subject to anxiety, fear, and fatigue.

- ☒ Digital obesity, synthetic relationships, and false perceptions of "true happiness" are creating a society where people want more out of life.

CHAPTER 2

GETTING YOUR PRIORITIES STRAIGHT

Time vs. Energy

Let's start out this chapter with a simple and straight-forward statement:

If you don't set your priorities... someone else will!

You might be wondering, "What does having priorities have to do with having purpose and passion?" It's because time is a commodity. You can't manipulate a 24-hour day. You have choices, and those choices will absolutely make or break your pathway to success. I've found that having total clarity around who or what is important in my life is the pathway to better decisions, focus, and the ability to live a life with intention.

When working with leaders, I often ask them to list their five to seven top priorities in life. It can be a person, a thing, an activity, you name it. Just tell me what's most important in your life so that we can take a closer look. That's really not that hard of an exercise.

We can all list things like family, friends, specific causes, work, or whatever. It's after we've discussed those most important people or things in their life that I ask them a much more direct question:

Force Rank Your Priorities

The key to force ranking is that there are no ties or caveats. I'm talking about full disclosure and clarity starting with numero uno and working your way down. Once we're done with that, the interrogation is only beginning. You see, where we spend our time and energy says a lot about whether we're living a life of intention. It speaks to our purpose and whether we're living a life of charades or truly locked in on our time as a spouse, parent, friend, co-worker, and so on, and it gives us clarity when faced with competing interests and priorities.

If you were to ask me to prioritize my life early in my marriage, I would have listed my wife and family as most important in my life. However, if you looked at where I spent my time and energy, about 60% was spent working and 20% was spent on a ball field or basketball court in my spare time. And while time spent with my wife and daughter was treasured... it wasn't close to being prioritized. While I might be over-dramatizing the fact that my life was not in sync, I certainly didn't have clarity, nor was I consistent. And while this is not an exercise to punish or make anyone feel inadequate during our journey of life, it is a time to help each of us to reflect on our "preferred future" and compassionately compare it to "reality." It's a time to step back regardless of what season of life you're in, and start living with consistency, make amends, and repair the imbalances of the past. It's a time to "force rank priorities" in order to make better decisions and realize that when faced with a choice, you really need to refer to the priorities YOU set.

You see, that's where you gain clarity and consistency. That's where you realize the importance of honoring and cherishing those most important in our lives. That's where you get in sync with your priorities, your energy, and your purpose!

But it's about this time during my coaching session where the leader says, "But you don't understand, I have to work long hours, travel, have multiple projects and deadlines with no grace or understanding about my personal life... I don't have *time*." And that's where I get to chime in with all of the humility I can muster and say, "Who said anything about time? You see, I'm talking about *energy*. I fully understand there's no way we can match a 50-60+ hour work week against the time needed to be a good husband/wife, a doting dad/mom, a caring friend, or a volunteer for a cause that moves you. However, we can replace time with energy!

Going back to the early years of my marriage, many hours were spent basically surviving life and getting through each week, and we weren't failing at time management, we were failing at energy. If you're a parent, you truly understand what I'm talking about. While our schedules were not time-friendly, we decided to make them "energy-friendly." We immediately started having date nights and set up a reciprocity system with the wonderful family that watched our daughter during the work week; they allowed us one night each week to ourselves, and we did the same for them by watching their children. And while three hours can't replace long work weeks, it can revive the lacking energy that was slowly depleting our relationship.

My wife and I have been happily married for 38 years, and the only advice we often give young couples is to devote energy to your relationship. Time is a commodity that gets sucked away from us with or without our permission, but energy can be the mere act of texting your spouse, child, or a friend during the middle of the day. A simple "Hope you're having a wonderful day. I love you!" is all the energy someone needs to know how much you care. While I worry about the effect that future technology will have on our well-being, it can also be just the antidote to keeping priorities and purpose intentional.

The Most Important Priority

As a leader, I've practiced the same process and paradigms that I ask of all leaders, including prioritizing my own priorities. When speaking, there's nothing I love more than to bait the audience to shout out what or whom they think my absolute number one priority is in life. Having read the last several pages, this is pretty much a slam dunk, right? My wife? My daughter? Family?

NO, emphatically NO. Are they at the top? You bet they are. In fact, my wife is a solid third on my priority list, and my daughter, whom I love like no other, comes in right behind at a whopping fourth. And while this might feel calloused and cold-hearted, I can at least tell you that my faith in Christ is at the top... yes, number one.

However, if you get nothing else from this book, please understand this one concept. The number two priority in my life is none other than ME! Yes, moi, me, numero uno, however you want to say it. Is it the ego talking? Is it pride and arrogance at work? Absolutely not! Even though this world will operate without a single glitch after the very moment I take my last breath, for me to honor and be the absolute best I can be and to take the best care of my wife, daughter, family, friends, and colleagues, I have to be at the top of my game every day for the rest of my life!

This is where the book takes a turn for a myopic focus on YOU. Yes, developing the best you that you can be so you have the energy and compassion to be your best-- with the sole purpose of taking care of those you love and honor the most. We have to be a little *selfish*... to be a whole lot of *selfless*. This is where transformation takes place and you truly start leading a **Rich and Intentional Life**! This is where the fun begins!

Just for clarity, my top seven priorities in life are:
1. Faith
2. Me (again, a little selfish to be a whole lot of selfless)
3. My wife (Sharon)
4. My daughter, her husband and family
5. Our wonderful friends
6. My colleagues at work
7. My hobbies and many, many interests!

Hopefully this gives you clarity into my earlier comments regarding how we make better decisions when we force-rank our priorities. Nothing comes between me and my faith. That's where my eternity lies. As I start every day, I immediately begin the selfish task of developing the muscles of mind (meditation), body (exercise), and soul (prayer and devotion). I do this to set the tone for the rest of the day with the mind-set of using all of my energy elevating, building up, and honoring others (more on morning routines in Chapter 10). By taking immaculate care of yourself, you can effectively honor and elevate others and begin living a **Rich and Intentional Life.**

After defining, force-ranking, and course-correcting your energy and priorities, the next step is to vividly think about someone delivering your eulogy as if your life has ended.

It's sad to think you will be the guest of honor for this event, but unfortunately, have no power regarding who attends, or more importantly, what is said. However, my biggest hope in life is that if those I prioritized most in life were asked to speak on my behalf, would their words be consistent with the priorities I set and the way I lived?

Therefore, this step involves asking you to merely write a short eulogy in the words of your spouse, significant other, children, family member, friends, colleagues, or anyone else you prioritized in life. Taking the time to do this is extremely important as you map out a plan for living a rich and intentional life. This process helps you mentally visualize your successful relationships while alive. It helps you develop and create intentionality towards your energy each and every day. It's something you need to read, review, and visualize daily or weekly as it will become reality.

As you've begun to see, my life is an open book. When speaking, I freely post my premeditated eulogy notes on screen in an effort to bring real life examples into the room. The illustration below conveys my desire of how to live as a dad and how I hope my daughter remembers me. This process, when reviewed daily and weekly, gave me the framework to both plan and instinctively act and react as a thoughtful and engaging father. It allowed me to fail and course-correct, often with her best interest in mind. Most importantly, this process gives me a road map for living with intention in all areas of my life.

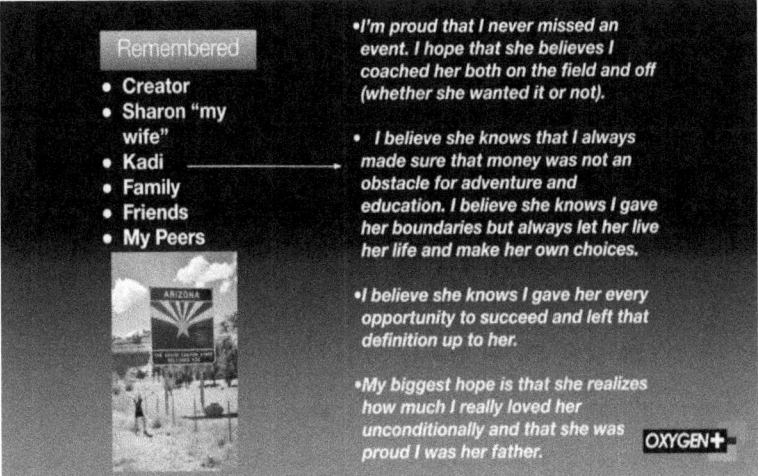

The processes in this chapter are used to develop clarity in life. Without clarity, we wander. We drift and chase shiny objects that lead to broken relationships, giving our time away, and eventually a life without meaning and intention. The only prerequisite to this exercise is an open heart, a little time, and a willingness to review frequently and visualize a life with intention.

Chapter 2 Key Concepts

- ☒ If you don't set your priorities, someone else will!

- ☒ Take care of you first! You need to be a little selfish so that you can in return be extremely selfless!

- ☒ It's not about time... it's about energy. Giving someone energy (even if it's texting, leaving notes, saying I love you a few times each day) will set the tone for honoring and living your priorities.

- ☒ Step 1: List five to seven people or activities that are most important in your life.

- ☒ Step 2: Force rank these priorities... no ties! This sets the framework for honoring priorities and making decisions.

- ☒ Step 3: Once you have force-ranked your priorities, create a separate column to list the "reality" of where you spend your energy. Are they in alignment?

- ☒ Step 4: Take the time to develop a eulogy through the eyes and words of those you've listed in your priorities. This becomes the script to the real life movie you want to live.

- ☒ Step 5: Review this script daily or weekly, and visualize this script as you meditate. It will become reality!

CHAPTER 3

KNOW WHO YOU ARE... AND WHO YOU'RE NOT

When working with leaders, without fail the first exercise is to make sure we know what our superpowers are, and more importantly... what they are not. We all covet for the personality or traits that we don't have. We all want to be the smartest person in the room or the one whom everyone continuously looks to for advice. The wonder drug "dopamine" goes off in our brain, giving us an emotional high when someone calls our name in a meeting, acknowledging our brilliance or yet another great point that we made. Inappropriate ambition is greed in disguise. Too many leaders let pride and ambition cloud their judgement and covet other leaders gifts. The truly respected are those who are comfortable and confident with their God-given design and have the patience to let their skills and gifts unfold.

Ray Dalio, former founder and CEO of Bridgewater, author of *Principles*, and one of the top thought leaders in the world said, "Because of the different ways that our brains are wired, we all experience reality in different ways, and any single way is, essentially, distorted. So if you want to know what to do about it, you must understand your own brain. That insight led me to talk with many psychologists, psychiatrists, neuroscientists, and personality testers. I discovered that though it is obvious to all of us that we are born with different strengths and weaknesses in areas, such as common sense, creativity, memory, synthesis, attention to detail, and so forth, examining these differences objectively makes even most scientists uncomfortable. However, I attribute as much of my success to what I've learned about my brain as I do to my understanding of economics and investing."

The bottom line is, YOU have gifts. You have superpowers! But knowing what those gifts and superpowers are and what they're not is far more important than being the smartest person in the room. You see, we're all wired uniquely. And while I long to be that person with the best ideas in the room… well, more times than not… it's not me! It's not that I'm inept or not well respected in my industry. It's not due to lack of preparation or IQ. It's just that my superpowers and contributions show up differently, and so do yours! As we go through this chapter, we'll explore different assessments that you and your team can use as you twist the rubik's cube together to develop **self-awareness.**

I believe that self-awareness, the recognition of your own character, feelings, motives, talents, and desire, is the least utilized but most important skill in leaders across America today. And, while many leaders have taken numerous assessments to understand their strengths and weaknesses, rarely does anyone truly understand how these superpowers can be a gift and a curse. Through various assessments, we've all been an animal, a number, a color, a shape, you name it. We all walked away with some affirmation of what we already knew, but mostly we walked away with anxiety toward what we're "NOT."

I once went through an exercise where my team took a personality profile assessment in advance of a full-day leadership exercise. Our individual leadership traits were put on a large poster sheet and put on walls around the room. However, names were missing from each of the poster sheets; the only things written on each sheet were merely traits and skills that each leader possessed. The sheets were anonymous, and our task was to guess whose name belonged on each sheet. Now mind you, I'm the head of real estate strategy for a Fortune 100 firm, and one of the sheets listed STRATEGIC, ANALYTICAL, and ACHIEVER among the traits. That's me, right? C'mon, throw me a bone; that suits me to a tee!

Well, while those might be part of my DNA, they really aren't my superpowers. In fact, those superpowers belonged to the relatively quiet and behind-the-scenes analyst who makes me look so brilliant. You see, my gifts and super powers are my ability to push others, make things better, identify talent, and communicate their brilliance to senior management. I have gifts of connecting dots but not the ability to think in multiple layers and process with the rich analytical depths of most on my team.

In fact, my gift (unknown to me at the time) was to hire a team from scratch with superpowers that fit the job at hand, and at times, allow me to synthesize their brilliance and communicate it in a way that only my superpowers can do so well. I had to come to some realizations several years ago that I may not be the smartest person in the room (and, normally, I'm not); however, I had the foresight and ability to fill the room with bright intelligent people with varying skills that gave our team unimaginably great results.

My advice to you, as leaders, is to get comfortable with your superpowers, focus and understand them, BUT DON'T LET THEM DEFINE YOU! Have a keen understanding and awareness of what gives you energy, drive, and focus, but also realize that you can "modify" weaknesses and personality traits over time with environment, routines, and visualization/meditation. Whatever superpowers you have are unique, and you should capitalize on them! Use them to your advantage, and know the superpowers of those around you. The key to assessments is their ability to analyze areas in life that energize you and your team, creating a beautiful orchestra of harmony and success. Embrace the results as they are merely pointing out where you have the most and least energy the "majority" of the time.

It's also important to understand that any muscle that's overworked or under-utilized can and will become a weakness. Let me give you an example: One of my gifts is that of an "Activator." I'm really skilled at getting action and inspiring others. I often have a vision in my mind, and immediately without hesitation, can connect dots and "let the party start." And while that skill allows me and my team to accomplish a lot, this skill can also create confusion, burnout, and solutions that could have been much better had I hit the breaks and asked others for input.

The mere thought of taking time and letting the idea be dissected by others only to be massaged to the point of inactivity absolutely zaps my energy. I'm probably off to the races with another idea or project.

However, this is the beauty of working on a team with multiple skill sets. While I get unquestionable energy working with leaders who mirror my personality and skill sets, we have the potential to get excited and react with a "fire, ready, aim" mentality. Therefore, you can see how important it is when working with leaders to make sure that we've dissected gifts and curses in order to minimize the barriers to results and success.

Let me introduce you to four assessments of which I'm sure you've either taken or are probably aware of:

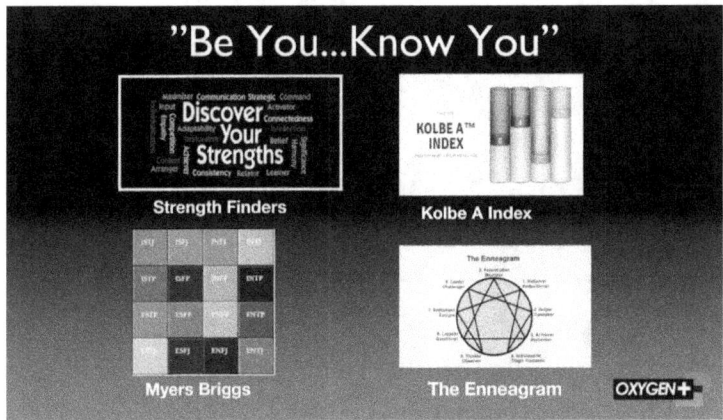

CliftonStrengths

The first (and more times than not, my "go-to") is Clifton-Strengths. This is a unique assessment where you identify 34 strengths (and areas with lower energy); however, the real crux of this assessment is the focus of your "top five gifts" or, as Clifton calls it, your "talent DNA." These top five are gifts that you were magically born with and give you energy each and every day. If you're using these five gifts the majority of the time, you've ultimately found the right job or pastime. This is nirvana for anyone, and you will find yourself living in "the zone." Listed below are the 34 gifts, and once you take the assessment, it will deliver your top five strengths and with an additional fee you can see your gifts 1 through 34 in descending order.

EXECUTING	INFLUENCING	RELATIONSHIP BUILDING	STRATEGIC THINKING
People with dominant Executing themes know how to make things happen	People with dominant Influencing themes know how to take charge, speak up, and make sure the team is heard	People with dominant Relationship Building themes have the ability to build strong relationships that can hold a team together and make the team greater than the sum of its parts	People with dominant Strategic Thinking themes help teams consider what could be. They absorb information that can inform better decisions
•Achiever •Arranger •Belief •Consistency •Deliberate •Discipline •Focus •Responsibility •Restorative	•Activator •Command •Communication •Competition •Maximizer •Self-Assurance •Significance •Woo	•Adaptability •Connectedness •Development •Empathy •Harmony •Includer •Individualization •Positivity •Relator	•Analytical •Context •Futuristic •Ideation •Input •Intellection •Learner •Strategic

As you can see, these gifts are divided into four buckets (Executing, Influencing, Relationship Building, Strategic Thinking), and you may be dominant in just one or have gifts across all four. Please stop reading and say aloud, "THERE IS NO RIGHT OR WRONG ANSWER." The absolute worst thing we can do with assessments is stress or covet another set of skills or gifts. What you have is absolutely beautiful! And with these five gifts comes energy. So, even though coveting other gifts may be natural, artificially acquiring these gifts will not give you energy, and in most cases, it will deplete what reserves you have.

Once you've taken the assessment, don't feel the urge to take it again. While it might change ever so slightly, the best thing to do is to know the sixth, seventh, or eighth gift and realize that given a different mood or set of circumstances, these gifts will and can give you energy as well. As you move down the list, you'll realize these gifts are better off lying within someone else's DNA, and if you really need them, you'll hang with them. And in most cases, they, too, will absolutely benefit from what you bring to the table.

As for me, my strengths are WOO (Winning Others Over), Activator, Maximizer, Arranger, and Communicator. Although I would LOVE to have strategic, analytical, focus and another dozen in my sweet spot, I'm the guy who casts a wide net and meets a lot of people. My personality is generally warm and people have an immediate trust with me. I love to make things better but rarely have the original idea. I can communicate concepts really well on stage or in a Powerpoint®, and I like to connect dots (Arrange and Activate) by putting together the right organizational chart or meshing the right personalities to form a team. While all of this sounds good, the dark and ugly side of me can think that these gifts are shallow. Who wants to be a WOO? Isn't that a synthetic and superficial salesman? Well, I hope not.

Even though I do have reservations about that label, I also realize I get tremendous energy from meeting new people and having a lot of close relationships. I don't know how it happens, but when I walk away from a conference or a meeting, I'm blessed to have found five new friends. It's these gifts that make me comfortable meeting other executives within our firm and spreading our brand throughout the company, and those on my team producing the secret sauce are more than happy to see me do my thing and expose their gifts. So, latch onto your top five (or six to eight) and realize this is where you get your energy. As mentioned before, I work with leaders to understand how when each of these gifts (muscles) is over- or under-used, they can and will become a curse or weakness.

As for those attributes that are at the bottom of your list, while you don't need to focus on them, DON'T let any of them become a career killer. If your job or brand requires you to "at least not suck" at one of these attributes, then address it, and make sure it doesn't drag you down. You don't have to master it, just make sure you have enough knowledge to not overshadow the skills and attributes that make you shine.

Kolbe A™ Index

For you sports geeks (I mean, enthusiasts) out there, you might be aware of the Wonderlic test created by Eldon Wonderlic. This 50-question test was created in the 30s and 40s and most recently used to test NFL athletes' cognitive skills in an effort to see whether they could process information fast enough to play in the ever-increasing sophistication of the NFL. There's plenty of evidence to see that this test is not necessarily the best indicator (i.e. Hall of Famers Dan Marino, Jim Kelly, and Terry Bradshaw basically flunked the test). In fact, one of the key critics of the Wonderlic test is Kathy Kolbe, the daughter of Eldon Wonderlic.

"I certainly value my father's work and there are many appropriate uses for it," Kolbe said. "I don't think it's a bad thing that the NFL uses it, I just don't think it's particularly wise.

"I think all the cognitive testing that happens in this country has gotten out of hand. My dad did a wonderful job back in the '30s and '40s creating the Wonderlic test at a time when we didn't have a good way of measuring cognitive skills and abilities for the workplace. But now the world has gotten into so much of this cognitive testing and people are over thinking and they believe how smart you are is so important to everything, and it's just not."

Kolbe goes on to say, "Unlike cognitive tests, the Kolbe A™ Index deals with the cognitive part of the brain but measures instincts and impulse rather than intellect. And in that area, there is no bias by gender, age, or race. It's a very different test in that there's no right or wrong. Instead, test-takers answer scenario-based questions in order to reveal personal strengths to potential employers. Personality tests are based upon preferences— what you want or wish you would do, and significant changes often occur in such results over time because of changes in your attitudes. Cognitive tests (IQ or skills) are not reliable over long intervals because you learn more and forget some of what you've learned; however, research shows that Kolbe A™ Index results are extremely consistent over time. Even after 15 years, more than 85% of people who retake the index have shown no significant changes in their Kolbe A™ results. No other measurement of human behavior has this high level of long-term retest reliability. It is only possible because the Kolbe A™ Index is a valid measurement of cognitive actions, and it identifies with your innate, unchanging, instinct-based strengths."

I have found that the Kolbe A™ Index is an excellent assessment to discover or affirm your natural talents and how to be most productive. Kolbe measures your instinctive way of doing things, and the result is called your MO (method of operation), and it can really help you understand your own human nature and begin the process of maximizing your potential.

The Kolbe A™ Index assessment consists of 36 questions. A supplemental report to the Kolbe A™ Index result, which identifies ways to use your instincts to make better decisions about money and finances, can be purchased for an additional fee. Each report includes a personalized path to financial success, and the assessment has an 82% accuracy rate, which is quite high when it comes to predicting human behavior. And with all assessments, there is NO WRONG ANSWER! This assessment is done in such a way that it actively promotes your work style, giving you all the reasons that your skills are extremely needed in various work environments.

There are four action modes in Kolbe A Index™: Fact Finder, Follow Thru, Quickstart, and Implementer. These are driven by instincts, and represent the primary ways we tackle challenges. The Kolbe Index™ measures them on a scale of 1-10, and respondents are labeled as Preventative (1-3), Accommodating (4-6), and Initiating (7-10).

For example, my Kolbe score was a 4-4-8-3.

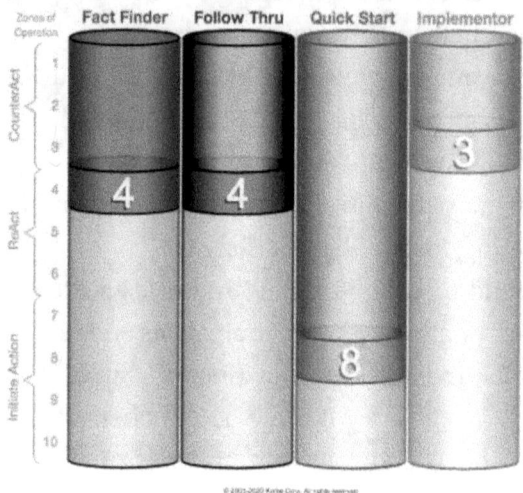

And, yes... it nailed me to a "T."

- I paraphrase, simplify, and explain, and I pull together information in a digestible manner (Fact Finder column).
- I'm somewhere in the middle of chaos and highly structured (Follow Thru Column). I'm the bridge between these two personalities. However, one comment in the assessment that got my attention is that I NEED self-imposed deadlines. While I knew this, it gave me insight as to how I need to structure my activities.
- From a Quick Start perspective, I'm the activator. I'm willing to take risks without having all of the facts. I love to take action! However, as I mentioned at the start of the chapter, our gifts can be a weakness if awareness is non-existent or

if we're not surrounding ourselves with those who complement our weaknesses.
- And finally, I imagine and visualize results (Implementor column). I deal with sensing vs. touching and feeling. I can learn more from a YouTube video than an owners manual. In addition, please don't ask me to fix appliances or work on my own car. My mind just doesn't process that way, and so I dearly "covet/admire" those who can!

In a nutshell, I do suggest you take the assessment individually or as a team. It really did give me insight and validation regarding my work style and intuitive nature. The results were much more in depth than what I provided in my summary. Why climb uphill if downhill is easier? Just knowing the difference and incorporating tools (i.e., planners, apps, etc.) to augment your gifts and/or minimize your weaknesses is the name of the game... and it's a whole lot more fun than taking the Wonderlic test!

Myers-Briggs

The Myers-Briggs Personality test has been on the shelf for several decades, but I still find it highly interesting and accurate. The Myers-Briggs Test Indicator (MBTI™) sorts people into one of 16 four-letter personality types based on their preferences for Sensing (S) or Intuition (N), Extraversion (E) or Introversion (I), Thinking (T) or Feeling (F), and Judging (J) or Perceiving (P).

ISTJ	ISFJ	INFJ	INTJ
ISTP	ISFP	INFP	INTP
ESTP	ESFP	ENFP	ENTP
ESTJ	ESFJ	ENFJ	ENTJ

This was my "go-to" personality test for years, and I still think it's highly useful when assessing what career might be most suitable for someone, as well as "how you or I respond when under stress." When speaking, I often refer to "Good Stan" and "Bad Stan." If I'm on a roll, keeping good routines, working out, eating well, and practicing most everything recommended in this book, I'm "Good Stan." My goal is to be "Good Stan" at least 85-90% of the time. Let's face it... none of us are "on" all of the time, but I'm passionate about staying in a healthy zone as often as possible by maintaining my physical, emotional, mental, and spiritual fitness. When I'm out of my routines, especially around the holidays, "Bad Stan" arises from the ashes, and the MTBI™ pretty much has me nailed!

So what stresses me out? According to MTBI™, I get stressed by unexpected change, uncooperative environments, and negative criticism. I dislike conflict with friends, family, or colleagues, and when I'm stressed, I tend to become pessimistic and inflexible. This self-awareness becomes extremely valuable, as I know and realize this isn't me. This isn't who I, or anyone else, want to be around. Obviously I need to course-correct and get back into the right routines. It may take several days or a week, but having self-awareness is critical!

I want to get back to "Good Stan." The charismatic optimist who finds the good in just about everyone. The jokester who is a strategic thinker pulling complex concepts together and loves to coach and bring out the best in others. Leaders **need** self-awareness and affirmation regarding "who they are... and who they aren't." All four assessments in this book are just samples of information out there to help us better understand ourselves, direct reports, peers, and family members. Having this knowledge gives us empathy and understanding when we develop the right teams and witness uncharacteristic behavior.

The MTBI™ has some age on it, and while they tout a 90% accuracy rating, there are scientific critics who dispel the MTBI™. The main criticisms frequently directed at the MBTI™ are: The types are only "stereotypes," and they do not describe individuals, and that the MBTI™ puts individuals in a box that does not allow a person to use a mix of the preferences. However, I'll continue to use the MTBI™ as an additional self-awareness tool that, when paired with other assessments, will give leaders a well rounded-view of your positive characteristics and behaviors under stress.

One final note, you can take a free version of the MTBI™ assessment online and/or a more thorough assessment for a fee. The latter version may be useful when researching ideal career options and more depth regarding learning behaviors and working under stress. In general, it's a great assessment that I still utilize today for various leaders depending on the outcomes we're working toward.

Enneagram

The Enneagram is an ancient personality system that identifies nine types of people and how they relate to one another and the world. The Enneagram is a powerful tool for understanding why we behave the way we do and how our personalities are powerfully influenced by our motivations. It provides a framework for how we can begin to live our most authentic selves, and it also reveals the wisdom each personality type can offer to others. Therefore, the Enneagram is not just a powerful tool for personal growth, but it's also a great resource for transforming our relationships in every sphere of life.

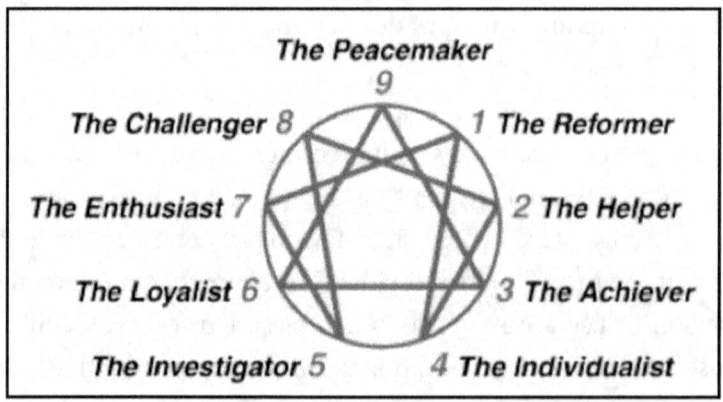

I strongly recommend you take this assessment because I believe it will open your eyes to its accuracy and further engagement in self-awareness. The test consists of 36 statements of opinion that you must rate on a five point scale of how much you agree with each. It should take most people 4-6 minutes to complete.

The nine personality profiles are:
1. *The Reformer* - The Rational, Idealistic Type:
   Principled, Purposeful, Self-controlled, and Perfectionistic
2. *The Helper* - The Caring, Interpersonal Type:

Demonstrative, Generous, People-Pleasing, and Possessive
3. ***The Achiever*** - The Success-Oriented, Pragmatic Type: Adaptive, Excelling, Driven, and Image-Conscious
4. ***The Individualist*** - The Sensitive, Withdrawn Type: Expressive, Dramatic, Self-Absorbed, and Temperamental
5. ***The Investigator*** - The Intense, Cerebral Type: Perceptive, Innovative, Secretive, and Isolated
6. ***The Loyalist*** - The Committed, Security-Oriented Type: Engaging, Responsible, Anxious, and Suspicious
7. ***The Enthusiast*** - The Busy, Fun-Loving Type: Spontaneous, Versatile, Distractible, and Scattered
8. ***The Challenger*** - The Powerful, Dominating Type: Self-Confident, Decisive, Willful, and Confrontational
9. ***The Peacemaker*** - The Easygoing, Self-Effacing Type: Receptive, Reassuring, Agreeable, and Complacent

Ian Cron, the author of *The Road Back To You*, has become my go-to source when researching the Enneagram. Ian is an Episcopal priest, best-selling author, psychotherapist, and Enneagram teacher. His book is an excellent resource for diving into each personality type, along with detailed descriptions of the personality types:

1) deadly sins
2) performance habits
3) relationship strengths
4) work styles
5) "wings" (each personality has some characteristic of two other personality types)

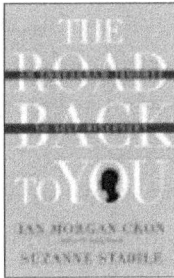

6) ability to deal with stress/security

7) spiritual transformation

8) paths for transformation

In addition to Ian Crone, there are wonderful podcasts specifically geared toward the Enneagram. A few worth mentioning are Enneagram & Coffee, Typology, and The Enneagram Journey.

As a proud "7," or better known as the Enthusiast, the Enneagram gives me further affirmation regarding how I act and react when healthy and/or unhealthy. In fact, at the time of this writing, it's very helpful as I, like many others, are quarantined during the COVID-19 pandemic of 2020. A "7" typically manufactures positivity and happiness, and when the cards aren't rolling right, well, then there is the flip side of avoiding pain, feeling somewhat sorry for myself, and believing I've been dealt a bad hand. As this unprecedented pandemic lingers on, I've sent several leaders whom I coach reminders of their Enneagram personality traits so that they can better understand their anxiety and reactions to challenges ahead.

In summary, the assessment tools I've mentioned (Clifton Strengths, Kolbe A™, Myers-Briggs, and the Enneagram) are nothing more than insight and self-awareness that merely affirm many things we already know and validate our behavior under stress and/or ideal situations. Knowing who you are... and who you're not, is critical as a leader, whether it's at work or at home. Having this insight into my relationship with my wife has been extremely helpful throughout our marriage. And for parents, having a tool like Myers-Briggs or the Enneagram can help shed light on what motivates and brings out the best (and sometimes worst) in our children, allowing us to have a little grace for the different styles we possess.

I've heard various life coaches degrade the value of assessments; however, I truly believe that if used correctly, and with the understanding that they are only tools for self-awareness, they can give us a baseline to optimally develop our strengths and help us see that overused strengths can become weaknesses that need to be recognized and developed.

Chapter 3 Key Concepts

- ☒ Know who you are... and who you're not! Be comfortable knowing that you are created with unique gifts that are even more valuable when paired with others' unique gifts.

- ☒ CliftonStrengths is an assessment that allows you to find five virtues (out of 34) that give you the most energy. You wake and go to bed with these five attributes, and they can serve you well as you navigate your career.

- ☒ The Kolbe A™ is an assessment that is best used to identify different work styles and form optimally-working teams. The Kolbe A™ deals with the cognitive part of the brain, measuring instincts and impulse rather than intellect.

- ☒ The Myers-Briggs assessment is a personality profile that sorts people into one of 16 four-letter personality types based on their preferences for Sensing (S) or Intuition (N), Extraversion (E) or Introversion (I), Thinking (T) or Feeling (F), and Judging (J) or Perceiving (P). It's highly effective for self awareness of when you're healthy and under stress. It's also a good tool for career development.

☒ The Enneagram is a personality typing system that identifies nine types of people and how they relate to one another and the world. The Enneagram is a powerful tool for understanding why we behave the way we do and how our personalities are powerfully influenced by our motivations.

MANAGING ENERGY

It's more Science than I thought

CHAPTER 4

A REASON FOR WAKING UP

Over the next four chapters, we'll explore what I believe to be the foundation for physical and mental well-being. The individual pillars of 1) Purpose, 2) Physical, 3) Emotional, and 4) Mental cannot stand alone. They should all work in concert, leaving you with energy and a feeling of purpose. This is the feeling of nirvana and "being in the zone." This is the state we want all leaders to experience every day for the rest of their lives.

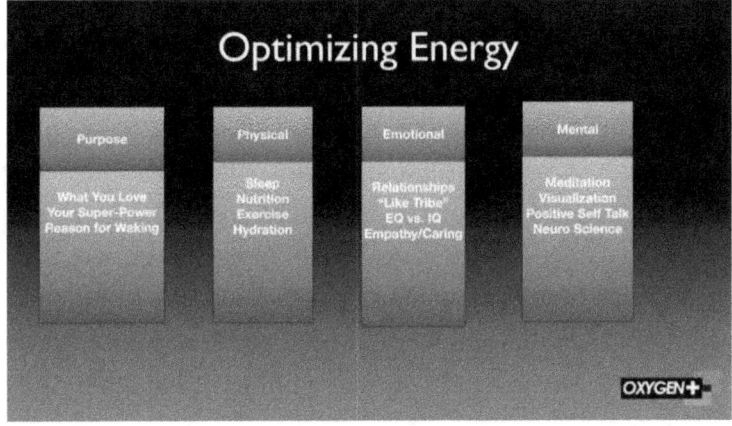

The first area to explore is Purpose. Several years ago, I asked a client whom I was coaching what mantra or prophetic saying has had an impact on his life, and his response resonated so deeply with me that I've continued to use it in my speeches over the last six years.

> The Dalai Lama, when asked what surprised him most about humanity, he said:
>
> Man...because he *sacrifices his health in order to make more money.*
> Then he *sacrifices money to recuperate his health.*
> And then he is so anxious about the future that he *does not enjoy the present*:
> the result being that he *does not live in the present or the future*:
> he lives as if he is never going to die, and then dies *having never really lived?*

When I deliver this quote in my speech, I repeat it twice. Once to let the meaning sink in and the second time for dramatic effect. Yes, it's really deep and deserves a moment of drama. You see, we really do spend our early life looking for purpose and working insane hours in an effort to make more money, and in the meantime, our youth slips away, and the quirks we used to mock our parents for take over in our personal lives. We put on unneeded weight and suddenly know what the upper and lower end of our blood pressure should be (typically because a doctor felt the need to explain it based on our results). Basically, we became adults who had no road map or exposure to Happiness 101 (but, I certainly couldn't get into Yale) and wonder what happened.

We then move into the phase of life where we know our doctor on a first name basis, and the nurse knows immediately to which pharmacy to send our prescriptions. In addition, we become "one" with our health care plan at work and never want to sign up for the more expensive plan, but... just to be safe, we can't bear the thought of spending what money we do have on the unexpected.

All of this leads us to start the phase of life where we say "uh oh... time's slipping by, and I don't have a plan." We are anxious about what the future holds and so preoccupied with it that we can't really enjoy the present. This preoccupation puts us in a panic attack, and while we think we'll never die... time slips by (pause for dramatic effect)... and we never really lived.

In the book *5 AM Club* by Robin Sharma, it states that some people die at 30 but are buried at 80. Well that's certainly a depressing thought! Over the last 50 years, the average lifespan has increased by about eight years, with women living until 81 and men approximately 76. However, it's beginning to stall and decline, as is quality of life, due to the increasing presence of muscle loss, obesity, osteoporosis, heart disease, cancer, and dementia.

In a *Wall Street Journal* article from January 14, 2020, titled "Heart Disease Strikes Back Across the U.S., Even in Healthy Places," author Betsy McKay notes, "Colorado is ranked as one of the nation's healthiest states. It often doesn't feel that way to David Rosenbaum. The Colorado Springs cardiologist regularly sees men and women in their 30s and 40s with heart problems, such as high blood pressure, irregular heart rhythms, and heart attacks. A visit from a young patient was rare when he started practicing there 17 year ago."

While this article references Colorado, by no means is Colorado different from a large list of states across the US. Some are worse than others; however, in today's world, we foster more stress and sedentary lifestyles than any generation before.

So now that I have your attention, and you probably just read a few comments from the Dalai Lama that hit a little close to home, the rest of this book will continuously dive into an integrated lifestyle consisting of physical, emotional, mental, and spiritual well-being. Within the spiritual well-being is the fact that living a rich and intentional life starts with having purpose. Purpose is the alpha behind every successful life. It's without doubt the first and foremost requested area clients want to explore. Purpose is as important to young adults as it is to those wanting to finish life strong and leave a legacy. Finding purpose is not easy and requires a deeper look within your soul and changes multiple times through life. However, there's nothing more gratifying than living the life you were meant to live, utilizing your God-given gifts, and waking up with a sense of confidence and peace from within.

Ikigai

I'm at a stage in life where people often ask when I want to ring the bell and settle into retirement. Personally, I couldn't think of anything worse! I'm an avid golfer, softball player, you name it... but a steady dose of any of my pastimes would never "fill my bucket" on any level! And when people tell me they are going to retire, I politely tell them to consider a new philosophy... Re-Focus.

In an article from the *British Medical Journal*, a study of Shell Oil employees showed that people who retired at age 55, and lived to be at least 65, died younger than people who retired at 65. After age 65, the early retirees have a 37% higher risk of death than their counterparts who retired at 65. Furthermore, people who retire at 55 are 89% more likely to die within the ten years after retirement than those who retire at 65. These statistics can be skewed given that we all come from different socioeconomic backgrounds, have different levels of education, and variable family medical history.

So let's throw statistics out the window for just a moment... I still can't think of anything worse than waking up each morning without a purpose. Say what you will about your professional life, but it still gives you structure and keeps you mentally stimulated.

You may be in a profession that fulfills your perfect design or it might be a stepping stone leading you to the next chapter of life. Regardless, you hold the keys to your personal happiness. I have yet to be in a job or profession where I didn't learn and make a choice to grow. Our financial systems have led us to believe that retirement starts as early as 62, with options to get additional benefits at 65 or later. Those are just numbers and have nothing to do with purpose and fulfillment. Purpose is "personal." It's about living a life that's rich each and every morning for as long as we're blessed to live.

In Japan, if you ask someone when they will retire, they would have absolutely no idea what you are referring to. You see, there is no word in the Japanese dictionary for retirement. Instead, the term they use, no matter what stage of life, is "*ikigai*." Ikigai in simple terms is a **reason for waking up**. Plain and simple, the Japanese culture values purpose and self-actualization in every phase of life. Similarly, the Costa Rican village of Nicoya uses the term "***plan de vida***." This term translates to "a reason to live" or "your soul's purpose."

Why are ikigai and plan de vida important? Because both terms are associated with cultures in the world where life spans often extend past 100 years of age. In fact, these people don't only live to be 100 in record numbers, but they display few of the stresses of modern-day society. These terms are specifically referenced in Dan Buettner's book called *The Blue Zone*. The "Blue Zones" are a collection of five areas in the world with the highest concentration of centurions (those who live past 100). Those five areas referenced by Buettners' team are:

- Okinawa (Japan) - *Home to the world's oldest women; they eat a lot of soy-based foods and practice tai chi, a meditative form of exercise*

- Nicoya Peninsula (Costa Rica) - *The Nicoyan Diet is based around beans and corn tortillas. The people of this area regularly perform physical jobs into old age and have a sense of purpose as noted above*

- Loma Linda (California/US) - *Mostly Seventh-day Adventists with strict vegetarian diets and live in tight knit communities*

- Ikaria (Greece) - *This is an island in Greece where they eat a Mediterranean diet rich in olive oil, red wine, and home-grown vegetables*

- Ogliastra (Sardinia/Italy) - *The Ogliastra region of Sardinia is home to some of the oldest men in the world. They live in mountainous regions where they typically work on farms and drink a lot of red wine*

The research shows that each of these cultures share nine common traits or themes that add to the quantity and quality of life. While I'm sure you locked into the fact that some love their red wine, the nine common themes are:

- They have a purpose in life
- Exercise is built in daily life
- They get plenty of sleep and rest
- They typically fast and/or eat until 80% full
- They eat a plant based diet
- They consume alcohol in moderation
- Engagement in spirituality or religion
- A strong sense of family
- A strong sense of community and engagement in the community

While this book is not about the Blue Zone Project, or how to live past 100 years of age, my findings from over 15 years of research are really no different. We need purpose or a reason to wake up. We need to eat well, rest, have strong relationships at home and within our community, and we have a need for spirituality. We'll touch on all of those in this book, however; if prioritizing the nine traits above, purpose continues to be the most consistent need for human beings at most every stage in life.

As noted by Abraham Maslow in his 1943 paper "A Theory of Human Motivation," three of the five basic needs for humans revolve around purpose and the need for belonging. Outside of physiological and safety needs, belongingness, esteem, and self-actualization are essential components to one's Ikigai or Plan de Vida.

Maslow's Hierarchy of Needs

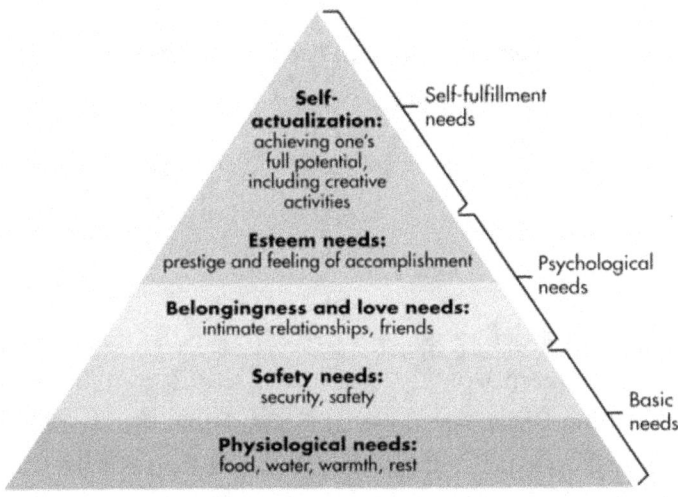

I have a friend who is a wonderful life coach named Paul Leavenworth (The Convergence Group). Several years ago, Paul shared a phrase with me that he found through his own research:

"From Success to Significance." That phrase resonated on many levels with me, as I've watched (and continue watching) many successful executives reach the ever-illusive phase of retirement only to see that their past success had very little bearing on their future happiness. They are lost, they want that sense of fulfillment that came from their position of authority. However, now they are turning the page and realizing there has to be more to life. Something that's fulfilling, and well… a reason to wake up in the morning.

Hector Garcia Puigcerver and Francesc Miralles further explored ikigai and wrote a book titled *Ikigai* in 2017. They noted that while some people find their ikigai quickly, others must seek it out over time. However, it's important to persist! It's important to find what gives you your energy. What is it that you enjoy so much that you can hardly wait for tomorrow to begin? I read a comment not to long ago that stated,

> *"If your job is your ikigai, don't retire, if it's your hobby, don't give it up, if you must retire… then refocus."*

To further define ikigai, Puigcerver and Miralles illustrate the four main themes of ikigai, as seen in the diagram below. Basically, 1) Doing What You Love, 2) Doing What the World Needs, 3) Are you Good At It?, and 4) Can You Get Paid For It?

Marrying these four ideologies together creates 1) mission, 2) vocation, 3) profession, and 4) passion. And when all of this comes together… you have your ikigai.

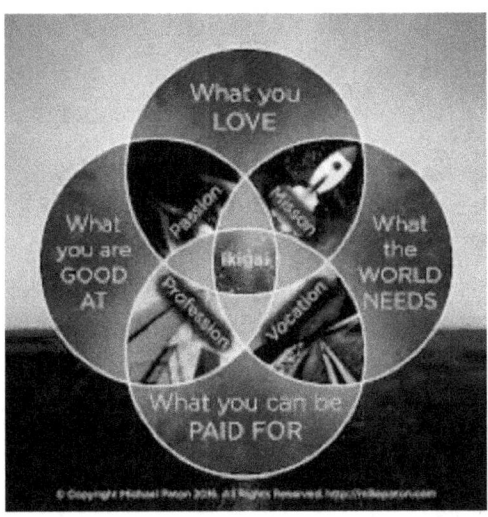

When speaking to audiences, I often reference two major themes regarding ikigai. First, your ikigai can change over time. My ikigai in my 20s and 30s was much different than my 50s and 60s. It will evolve, and you should allow it to evolve.

The second key point is that your ikigai doesn't necessarily have to make money (i.e. what can you be paid for). If you take payment out of the equation, you are quite simply left with "a hobby." Hobbies can definitely be your ikigai assuming you become good at it, you love doing it, and the world needs it. My practice of public speaking, writing this book, and leadership development yield very little income at this stage of my ikigai. As mentioned in my foreword, I still work a full time job that I really enjoy, yet, I have the time to pursue my passion and career as a national speaker.

In a 2010 survey of 2,000 Japanese men and women, just 31% of participants cited work as their ikigai. While I still believe work is very much integrated into one's purpose, the point is, you can have more than one reason to wake up in the morning. And from my perspective, what's wrong with having multiple passions in life and using your God-given talents to make your and others' lives more complete!

So my advice to you is to always be searching and clarifying your reason to wake up (purpose). Explore your natural gifts (see Chapter 3) and core values (see Chapter 9), define your priorities and mission in life and never... I mean never... settle for mediocrity. Listed below are some questions when looking for your purpose. I captured these from another coach (Julie Smith, The Success Factor) and found them very useful:

- Can it impact others in a positive way?
- Is it enduring? Will it create a legacy outliving my time on earth?
- Will it integrate into all areas of my life? Does it touch my family, work, friends and colleagues? Can my purpose be bigger than "me?"
- Is it inspiring to YOU? Does it deeply motivate you and get you through the tough times?

And be mindful for what your purpose isn't. It's not:

- A job, a role or a relationship
- It's not necessarily magnificent or earth shattering
- It's not immediate, and often it is a process that needs to unfold. I often tell my clients that purpose is the journey... not the destination. Whatever goal you set will only be met with another mountain to reach. However, the journey is what you will remember.

As for me and my ikigai, I've settled into a simple but daunting purpose.

"I am a Christ follower who wants to elevate, transform, and inspire over 100,000 people to live a rich and intentional life. I want to coach, teach, connect, and lead others to greatness."

I have no metric to measure my success. However, I know that my purpose will challenge me as an author when speaking to audiences from all walks of life, mentoring, and providing leadership development and seminars to anyone wanting to seek their ikigai. And quite honestly, when I see that look of hope and success in just one client's eyes, my ikigai is full, and I know I'm waking each morning with passion and purpose.

Chapter 4 Key Concepts

- ☒ Over the last 50 years, the average lifespan has increased by about 8 years, with women living until 81 and men approximately 76. However, it's beginning to stall and decline, as well as the quality of life. Muscle loss, obesity, osteoporosis, heart disease, cancer, and dementia are becoming all too common as we age.

- ☒ Ikigai is the Japanese phrase for "a reason to wake up" or purpose. There is no word for retirement in Japanese... just a culture for having purpose.

- ☒ *The Blue Zone* is a book written by Dan Buettner and his research team, which identifies five cultures around the world where people live past 100 (centurions).

- ☒ There are nine common themes these Blue Zone cultures have in common. Purpose is noted to be one of the most important.

- ☒ To find your ikigai or purpose, find what you love, what you are good at, what the world needs, and what you can get paid for.

- ☒ If your ikigai or purpose doesn't involve compensation, it's a hobby... and that's ok!

- ☒ Your purpose can and will change over time. Each quarter of life will probably yield a new purpose or reason for waking up in the morning.

CHAPTER 5

THE PHYSICAL SIDE OF LIFE

This chapter looks at the physiological benefits of sleep, exercise, nutrition, and hydration. While mind, body, and soul are the key tenets to personal development, I firmly believe that when the body is operating and feeling optimal, you then have the energy to address the mind and the soul and take your life to a new level. While all four areas are extremely important, they are prioritized in the order I believe give you the greatest lift. If you aren't well rested (sleep), your energy levels are low and making good nutritional decisions become harder. And if you aren't eating well, exercise becomes more taxing and results are not as efficient. And while getting a good night's sleep, eating well, and exercising are critical for living a rich life, all areas of the body will only function as God intended when properly hydrated.

This chapter is a lifestyle. It's about making small changes (routines) in order to see epic results and give you the energy to make changes in all areas of your life. The decisions we make today are directly related to the quality and quantity of existence. In the previous chapter, the Dalai Lama was quoted "We sacrifice our health in order to make more money... and then sacrifice money to recuperate our health." Again, small changes in sleep, nutrition, exercise, and hydration can and will lead to epic results in your journey to greatness.

Sleep

Much of our energy is jettisoned by the quality of our sleep. At the risk of my editor telling me I can't continue to put sentences in BOLD... let me repeat, "**Sleep is absolutely the foundation**" for leading an intentional life. If we don't feel well, if we're not rested and we're tired, we simply don't have the energy to do anything else. That includes eating right, exercising, working, developing our minds, you name it.

What really fascinates me is the science and physiological effects that sleep deprivation have on the body. In short, most resources will tell you that between seven and eight hours of sleep is optimal. Anything less or more (more is defined as nine plus hours) for 99% of our population will either put us in a sleep deficit or fatigue. A few of the physiological effects of sleep fatigue are:

- Inability to break down glucose, causing diabetes/obesity
- High blood pressure
- Heart disease
- Cognitive impairment
- Slowed physical recovery

Don't kill the messenger but just Google or research any sleep specialist and you'll find the same results. I often give this cautionary tale of cognitive impairment: For every hour of sleep less than seven hours, you basically lose one point of IQ. That's hardly anything to worry about. However, that number multiplies exponentially each day you continue to sleep fewer than seven hours. For example, day two equals two IQ points, day three equals four, day four equals eight, day five equals 16. You get the point. After about a week of sleep deficit, you're operating on an IQ that's roughly 30-40% less than what you are capable of. And while this is what science tells us, I know that I've operated in a deficit and still been able to perform over a week's time, but the fact is that it's not ideal; it's affecting your ability to work, live, and process information optimally.

A lot happens to our brains and our bodies while we sleep. When we get our ZZZ's, we cycle between REM and non-REM sleep. REM, which stands for Rapid Eye Movement, is the stage in which your eyes move quickly in different directions. REM sleep is associated with our "dream state" and typically happens 90 minutes after you fall asleep and occurs periodically throughout the night. During our REM or dream state, our brain is actually much more active than when we're awake. Our optimal REM/dream state is typically around 20-25% of our total duration of sleep, while babies can be in REM state for 50% of the time.

While in REM, the neurons in the brain shrink by as much as 60% when the cerebral spinal fluids wash through the brain much like a car wash. The brain is essentially washing away all of the non-important information you deem essential, giving our brains more capacity for the day ahead.

My wife and I measure our REM nightly via our smart watches, and I'm ashamed to say it's probably the first question we ask each other after waking. We're shooting for one and a half to two hours of REM nightly and often do a "look back" at our nightly routines to monitor when we've slept well (i.e., no food or wine three hours before bed, lower the lights/LED to produce melatonin one to two hours before bed, etc.).

Another note worth mentioning comes from the book titled *The 5 AM Club*, in which the author, Robin Sharma, talks about the Human Growth Hormone (HGH). HGH is produced in the pituitary gland of the brain and is important for healthy tissues in your body, a strong functioning metabolism, and a long life span (some pretty important stuff there). Increased levels of HGH raise your moods, cognition, energy levels, and lean muscle mass, and reduce your cravings through the regulation of leptin and ghrelin. The main point is that while HGH is released through exercise, 75% is released when you sleep! And to back up the earlier point of needing seven to eight hours of sleep, science is telling us that to release HGH and properly wash the brain, we need five complete ninety-minute sleep cycles, which magically comes up to seven and a half hours of sleep for adults.

I would be remiss as well if I didn't talk about melatonin when discussing sleep science. Melatonin's main job in the body is to regulate night and day cycles, or sleep-wake cycles. Darkness increases melatonin production and signals the body that it's time to sleep. So our early ancestors who lacked the modern conveniences that we now enjoy (LED lighting, computer and phone screens, etc.) had natural sleep cycles as the sun went down. However, we prolong the production of melatonin by keeping our lights on, binge watching television, and especially, checking our digital devices until the time we plan to sleep.

In my opinion, that is without a doubt the quickest way to ruin a good night's sleep. Some people take melatonin to help speed up the process and produce a quicker and deeper way to slumber.

However, not many, if any, sleep science doctors would recommend this, and if they do, they would recommend natural products and very low doses of two to five mg and only as a supplement to other good sleep rituals.

One key to good sleep is the development of evening routines designed to enhance the parasympathetic nervous system, which inhibits the body from overworking and restores the body to a calm and composed state (more on the parasympathetic nervous system as we discuss routines in Chapter 10).

To track our sleep, my wife and I use a sleep app on our Apple watches, called AutoSleep. And while sleep apps aren't perfect, they can be directionally correct and give you enough data to work towards an optimal sleep routine. Other products that I'm monitoring are an attractive ring you wear on your finger called Oura and a bracelet called WHOOP, which measures deep sleep, REM, light sleep, and how quickly you fall asleep. Sleep headbands are also popular, such as the Muse headband, which offers meditation and sleep sensors for a more holistic approach.

However, if you suffer from serious long-term periods of sleep deprivation or merely wanting optimal sleep, I would strongly suggest you see a sleep doctor or coach specializing in sleep science as there are many devices and practices aimed at optimal sleep. I have a friend, Patrick DeNicola, who is a sleep specialist who coaches clients to find greater levels of performance and productivity through sleep mastery. While Patrick has several methods that make his practice successful, he recently shared with me a fascinating technique he implemented for a client who was filled with evening anxiety and no remedy to fall asleep. Patrick's story goes like this:

"Over the years of perfecting my practice, I have come across a very specific problem when it comes to sleep that for some can become a very infuriating disconnect. You see, I have developed a system designed to serve as a guide to maximize recovery and enhance overall energy. This system is built on a few foundational principles that apply not only to improving sleep but also the individual creating a healthier more vibrant being. So for example, nutrition is a vital part of my program; detoxifying the body of harmful toxins and chemicals create a huge step towards increased performance and recovery, and thus, sleep. Some of these principles are shared with other healers and coaches as the path towards greater health, and abundance is a shared experience, meaning no matter your goal in improving your health, there are certain practices and beliefs that will unify all of these healing methods.

"As I was building these systems and working with individuals, I found there was a big missing piece to this sleep pizza pie. It wasn't until I discovered this hidden opportunity that I became fully confident in my ability to help thousands improve their lives without making life such a complicated and ritualized process. This discovery came from a problem. It came as an answer, in a flash, as I was diving into a session with a client as we were laying the groundwork of the system he would follow. As a performance coach, I have found myself working with mostly entrepreneur types. My client was communicating sleep practices he has tried in the past to no avail, of which I would not have recommended. He tried different techniques and practices to quiet the mind, and yet, the problem still persisted. He explained it like this, 'It's like I spend my whole day working on my business, working towards my goals, checking off of the boxes towards success. But as I wind down to reflect on the day, meditate, eat, etc., my mind becomes a beacon of creativity, and three or four hours later, I'm finally able to let it all go, fall asleep, and repeat the next day. Admittedly, I'm not getting the rest I need. What else can I do?' The light bulb hit me, a flush of insight overcame me, and I responded with the diagnosis that has led to a better understanding of the problem and solution. I simply replied, 'Our bodies are energetic in nature, meaning that the entirety of our being is a bioenergetic being. And when we look at the body on the quantum subatomic level, we see mostly nothingness, an empty space between the atoms. This empty space is not actually empty, but a container of pure potential energy. Taking this equation from the small and applying it to the big allows for us to begin to understand *the body is one of energy and electricity*. We also have centers in the body that help move our bodies' energy into the proper places at the proper times to perform our necessary functions. Each energy center has a specific purpose, and the centers are known as chakras in the east and detected by modern science.' So what's happening here? What does the fact that we are energy with energy centers have to do with sleep? The answer is that your energy is getting stuck in the higher centers. The energy is getting stuck in the active regions of your consciousness, and thus, because you haven't learned how to bring these energies down through the body and out of the mind, you stay alert and shift into this creative mode of thinking. So, what is needed is for you to learn how to shift your energies down into physical centers, thus, freeing the burden on your mind to stay active."

Enter into the discussion: My realization of the importance of a very ancient practice. One that humans have been knowingly or unknowingly practicing for all of our existence, except for these last 100 years in the western world. The practice of grounding the body (a.k.a. "earthing"). It's amazing what grounding can do for this specific problem or similar issues of neural activity keeping you awake, restless, and without sleep. Grounding is touching your bare feet to the earth– which, over the last 20 years has had immense significance to health and wellness across the board. When you ground before sleep, the body intuitively knows it's time to shut down, relax, and let go. Spending just five minutes with this practice will signal to your body the necessity of letting your energy drop and center itself within the body. This practice centers your energy via the response to the connection with the earth, which is useful as you wind down before your intended bed time.

Ironically, it has the exact opposite effect in the morning as an energizer by organizing the energy of the body to uplift and excite. I could write about the benefits of grounding for hours. So, I implore you to try it out and see if this simple daily practice has the same effect it has had in myself and countless others (*Author's note: check out Earthing.com for several grounding products related to sleep, recovery, and everyday use; in addition, try grounding with the earth at least 30 minutes each day and thoroughly research the pros/cons of indoor grounding*).

Another resource for sleep efficiency that I often refer to is Dr. Matthew P. Walker, who is the Professor of Neuroscience and Psychology at the University of California, Berkeley, and Founder and Director of the Center for Human Sleep Science. I find his YouTube channel and articles on sleep to be a wealth of information as it relates to the science of sleep, optimal routines, and various methods to maximize your sleep cycle. Another book worth mentioning is *Sleep Smarter* by Shawn Stevenson. This book has 21 essential strategies to sleep your way to a better body and better health.

Nutrition

As I talk about physical energy (sleep, nutrition, exercise, and hydration), I list nutrition as the second most important area of focus even though it could arguably be number one. Hippocrates once so wisely quipped in 300 B.C., "Let food be thy medicine or medicine be thy food." While there are many natural and unnatural causes for diseases, a few controllable and uncontrollable causes are:

- Environmental (i.e., pesticides, etc.)
- Viruses (i.e., SARS, Ebola, Coronavirus)
- Stress (stress weakens the immune system, which is the gateway to sickness and disease)
- Nutrition

And while this is not an exhaustive list, I can tell you unequivocally, nutrition is by far and away the leading cause for sickness and disease. On the positive side, nutrition and stress are two things that you and I can control.

In this segment, I will not tell you what diet is best for you since our hormonal systems are all different and unique. In fact, I despise the word "diet" because I desire a sustainable plan that I can live with for the rest of my life. I will, however, give you what I believe to be good practices and the physiological effects that food and our gut bacteria have on our body. In addition, I will suggest that you find a doctor who specializes in micronutrient testing, which is next-generation testing in an effort to measure specific vitamins, minerals, antioxidants, amino/fatty acids, and metabolites within your white blood cells.

I've come to the conclusion that God created us differently, similarly as none of us have the same fingerprints. For that reason I truly believe that we need some trial and error in our quest for a sustainable nutrient plan that gives us abundant energy and quality of life. If you're interested in micronutrient testing (or precision medicine), I would recommend 'Wild Health Podcast,' which is hosted by Dr. Matt Dawson and Dr. Mike Mallin. They offer genomics-based personalized medicine by analyzing your genome, lifestyle, lab results, and goals to optimize your health.

PCF

Several years ago, my wife and I ran across a very interesting lady who lives on an island, not too far from us, on the gulf coast of Florida. Her name is Diana, and she looks to be in her late 40s or early-mid 50s. Her past includes working at Coopers Medical Institute in Dallas, Texas, and she now lives on the island and spends her time teaching yoga, growing her own food, and giving advice on nutrition. What surprised us as we got to know her is that she's really in her early-mid 70s and is either blessed with a great gene pool or she really knows something the rest of us don't. For that reason we decided it was worth our money to sit down and ask for her advice on the fountain of youth.

She started off by telling us that she believes stress is 85% directly related to disease, which is a reversal from nutrition being the culprit, as I mentioned earlier. However, eating and meditation can reduce stress and, with her next breath, she quickly recited three letters... P.C.F.. And while I was hoping that was short for pizza, Coke, and fries, I quickly found out that her nutritional advice is centered around protein, carbs, and fat.

As we talked further, it is her belief that our protein should be approximately 15% of our overall diet. And, of course that would be the leaner proteins in life, consisting of fish (wild salmon), chicken, lamb, and eggs, and also hemp seeds and 2% cottage cheese. As for carbs, she was quick to give us the phrase, "Five is fine but nine is divine." By that she meant we should get five to nine cups of carbs daily because they should represent approximately 60-70% of our food plan. These carbs include vegetables (broccoli, brussel sprouts, cauliflower, and cabbage), fruits, pure brown rice, and durum wheat pasta, just to name a few. She also mentioned that our veggie to fruit ratio should be about 2:1 in an effort to minimize sugar; and as for fat, we basically need "good" fat to burn fat. Good fat can be found in nuts (also protein), avocados, organic butter, and olive oil.

Her final comment was that carbohydrates leave our body in roughly 30 minutes, and protein stays with us for three hours, and "good" fats will last for six hours. Keeping this in mind, her belief is that we should "eat to thrive and stay full," which is different from the increasingly popular science around intermittent fasting (more on that later). And fortunately, Diana added that dark roasted coffee and kombucha are great additions to our daily nutrition habits.

As I assessed Diana's advice, I really came to the conclusion that it mirrors the Mediterranean Diet, which is also the diet endorsed by Mayo Clinic. Whatever your choice is, make sure it's sustainable and leaves you energized and comfortable. The Greek philosopher Plato believed he was once given the ultimate compliment after his dinner party when a guest said, "I not only enjoy your meals, I enjoy the way they make me feel the day after."

Intermittent Fasting

I also mentioned intermittent fasting (IF). And while I have researched the science and believe this to be not only a good way to minimize caloric intake, I also believe it has a physiological benefit as a result of the basic concept that you alter the various cycles of eating and fasting. It does not dictate *which* foods you should eat, but rather *when* you should eat them. That said, it is often accompanied by a low-carb diet, and together they help you lose weight and keep your blood sugar and insulin levels stable.

One of the key theories of intermittent fasting is that the fasting period controls the hormone insulin. Controlling insulin requires a change in our diet, which is composed of two factors – how high the insulin levels are after meals, and how long they persist. Therefore it boils down to two simple factors:

1. What we eat - determines how high insulin spikes
2. When we eat- determines how persistent insulin is

There are many different types of intermittent fasting, and the most popular plan is to skip breakfast and eat between the hours of noon and 8:00 P.M., which is called the 16:8 plan. Another plan is to fast two days per week allowing 500 calories for women and 600 for men on fasting days. The final plan is called the One Meal A Day (OMAD) plan, which consists of eating a large and satisfying meal once per day.

And instead of going into the mounds of science around IF, I believe you will get a lot of great advice on the internet, and I believe it's worth mentioning to and getting advice from your doctor. One doctor who is an advocate for IF is Dr. Jason Fung. I find his YouTube clips and online articles to be fascinating and full of common sense. He is a Canadian nephrologist and a world-leading intermittent fasting expert who specializes in treating people with Type 2 diabetes, and he is also the author of the book *The Obesity Code*.

A final comment on IF is that during the fasting period, you can (and should) drink fluids including water, tea, lemon-water, apple cider vinegar, and coffee. And while you may get a little hungry during the first few weeks, IF becomes the norm, and because of the fat-burning process while fasting, one of the benefits is increased energy. As you read more about IF, you will see several claims for benefits including cleansing of cells, weight loss, lowered inflammation, and focus; and while there are many benefits, it is also important to note that intermittent fasting is still a science under review and not designed for individuals under 18, pregnant women, people with Type 1 diabetes or those recovering from surgery.

The Gut

The next area to explore is the gut... yes, the stomach. The gut is now becoming known as the "second brain." The stomach has a direct link to our inflammation system, heart, and brain, and of course, what we put in our (mouths and) stomachs has a direct effect on our health and our ability to ward off sickness and disease.

As we explore the gut, I will often refer to Dr. Steven Gundry whose book *The Longevity Paradox* lays out three of the most crucial factors behind aging well: our gut bacteria, our gut walls, and our mitochondria. Dr. Gundry founded and runs the International Heart and Lung Institute and the Center for Restorative Medicine. Other great books to research are *Gut* by Giulia Enders and *Eat to Beat Disease* by William W. Li.

In everyone's quest to look and feel younger, we don't need to look any further than our digestive systems. While we all wish for good family genes, the genes that have the biggest bearing on your longevity aren't the ones inside your human body cells; they're the ones inside the single-cell bacteria that live within, on, and in the air immediately surrounding your body. There are trillions of these bacteria, and they come in different species. Some of these bacteria are good for your longevity; others are bad. So while one type of gut bacteria called Escherichia can cause inflammation, Eubacterium Rectale can help combat it. And, chronic inflammation is NOT our friend. It can lead to a range of diseases that tend to come with aging (i.e., inflammation of the brain leads to Parkinson's Disease, Alzheimer's and dementia). We'll touch more on inflammation in the next section, titled "Exercise," but it's critical to know that stress and various foods can add to inflammation, which lowers our immune system and leads to aging, sickness, and disease.

So, one of the keys to longevity is therefore nourishing your good bacteria and starving your bad bacteria. That's where a healthy diet comes into the picture. One way to nourish your good bacteria is to consume plenty of foods that provide sources of prebiotics, which are substances that promote the bacteria growth (that's good!). Some great sources of prebiotics are yams, fungi (such as mushrooms), and roots (such as turnips).

Conversely, to starve your bad bacteria, you need to avoid the substances they like. Unfortunately, one of their favorite things to chomp on is sugar – and not just the table sugar in deserts, but the sugar in fruits, too. Grapes, pineapples, and ripe bananas are loaded with sugar called fructose, of which your "bad" bacteria loves.

Also of importance is the mitochondria. This is important because the mitochondria is essential for taking nutrients and substances that have been processed by our gut bacteria and converting them into energy for our cells. In addition, they decide how quickly our cells should grow, which ones should live, and which ones should die. So the mitochondria, in collaboration with our gut bacteria, is critical to the aging process. For that reason, we want to give our mitochondria good food (and exercise). Of those foods, nuts – especially walnuts, pistachios, and almonds – feed the mitochondria and are a wonderful source of protein. Maybe Diana from Florida is on to something? Conversely, meat that contains iron disrupts the mitochondria's ability to produce energy by lowering their oxygen level.

Finally, we'll talk about the third piece of the triangle, the gut wall. This is the protective barrier between your gut and the rest of your body. It's a single layer of mucus-producing cells that line your intestines. Why is this important? Your gut wall and its immune cells decide which bacteria to let through and which ones to keep out. If all goes well, the rest of the body gets the nutrients and other beneficial substances it needs. And, there are some bad guys, such as lipopolysaccharides (LPSs), that we don't want to get through the gut barrier. Trillions of these LPSs get produced every day— which is an ominous fact, given how harmful they can be if they breach your gut wall and reach your blood, organs, tissues, and lymphatic system (part of the immune system we discussed earlier). When LPSs start to slip through, the rest of your immune cells come to the defense and react accordingly, which leads to inflammation. If that happens over and over, it's called chronic inflammation, and it is one of the ultimate causes of many of the most common ailments associated with aging, including diabetes, osteoporosis, arthritis, cancer, and Alzheimers.

So, it's critically important to know what we're putting in our bodies and the fact that we have trillions of bacteria floating around, some of which we like and some... well, they're leading us down a path we don't want to go. Be cognizant of the typical western diet. It's loaded with processed foods, sugars, lectins (found in grains such as rice and wheat), excessive alcohol, and anti-inflammatory drugs (i.e. ibuprofen and Advil) which can actually cause more damage to the gut wall. Instead, consume a good diet (see previous comments regarding Diana from Florida), including eating a diverse range of foods (legumes, beans, and fruit containing fiber). Eat fermented foods, such as yogurt and sauerkraut. Limit your intake of artificial sweeteners, and eat more prebiotic foods, such as artichokes, asparagus, oats, and apples, and consume whole grains that contain a lot of fiber, and beneficial carbs that are easily digested by the gut bacteria to promote overall good health.

Additionally, you can take a probiotic supplement of live bacteria, which can help maintain a beneficial balance of good bacteria in the gut. And now for my favorite part, drinks that contain polyphenols (think berries, grapes, and moderate amounts of red wine) are excellent at controlling your gut wall, along with moderate amounts of strength training and cardiovascular exercise.

While I'm not a doctor and have no desire to start that process, the research, knowledge and nutrient testing (i.e., micronutrient and 21 SMACK blood test) is limitless. And, it might seem complex, but it's really not. There is no one right system for everyone, but there is a better system for you. It just needs to be sustainable, natural, and if we do go off the rails, it's just an event and not a practice.

My ask is that you research and realize that the wrong foods play a large role in inflammation, stress, disease, and aging. We don't have to be perfect, but we need to make changes if we truly want to have optimal energy and live a quality life with abundant energy.

Exercise

I've listed exercise and fitness behind sleep and nutrition. However, make no mistake, when it comes to energy, movement is without a doubt one of the most critical things we can do. And back to our centurion friends in the Blue Zone who live past 100 years of age, movement is one of the nine common traits to living a long life. Movement isn't necessarily a five-mile run or an intense program to reshape your body. No, movement, for me, is an opportunity to get my brain wiring and firing. It's the ability to exercise our heart and keep our body functioning as long as possible. The motivation for me to move five to six days a week is more about the brain and the heart and less about the shape of my body. As I go through this chapter, I'll introduce the key physiological and psychological effects that movement has on the quantity and quality of our lives.

The research I will reference most in this chapter, of which I think does an excellent job listing the physiological and psychological effects of movement are 1) *The 5 AM Club* (which I've already noted in prior chapters) and 2) *Younger Next Year* Live Strong, Fit, and Sexy-Until You're 80 and Beyond*. Younger Next Year* is written by Chris Crowley and Henry S. Lodge, M.D. It's hilariously written, yet packs all of the science needed to motivate you to exercise.

Let me first start out by saying that reshaping our body is as much about nutrition as it is exercise. If you want to lose weight, nutrition will give you the results much faster than walking, jogging, or whatever form of fitness you choose. Calorie reduction comes much easier when eating well than from a one hour workout that burns a total of 200-400 calories.

However, the two work together beautifully! Combining nutrition and fitness will transform the body, strengthen the heart, tone the muscles, and provide natural neurological and mood benefits, lasting a lifetime. However, what (and how much) you eat and the type of exercise you do will dictate the shape and health of your body. For example, if you eat a lot of junk food and power lift (weights), you will gain muscle but not an optimal physique. And, if you don't get the appropriate nutrition you need or exercise, you'll lose muscle mass and become fatigued, and experience increased illness or infection and feelings of depression. So please note, I've written Chapter 5 to include the entire package of sleep, nutrition, fitness, and hydration as they all work together in an effort to deliver abundant energy and quality of life.

In the book *The 5 AM Club*, author Robin Sharma unequivocally stresses the need to jump out of bed and get the heart rate going. He states, "Doing some sweaty exercise first thing in the morning will revolutionize the quality of your days. Moving vigorously shortly after you get up will generate an alchemy in your brain – based on its neurobiology – which will not only wake you up fully, but electrify your focus and energy, amplify your self-discipline, and launch your day in a way that makes you feel on fire." It regulates the amygdala in the limbic system, the almond-like shaped nuclei in our brain that helps regulate focus, emotion, and behavior, allowing us to gracefully navigate hard projects and the difficult situations that used to upend our day. It also lowers our cortisol, the hormone of fear (housed in your adrenal glands) and releases it into your bloodstream, which is highest in the morning, and sets you up for a calmer and more optimal day. In addition, BDNF (brain-derived neurotrophic factor) is released, which has been shown to repair brain cells damaged by stress and accelerate the formation of neural connections. Dopamine (which regulates drive) and serotonin (which regulates happiness) is released, enhancing your mood. Exercising first thing in the morning also elevates your metabolism and fuels the fat-burning engine of your body so you burn any excess more efficiently. The benefits of starting out the day with some elevated activity and motion is mind-boggling and truly sets the pace for the rest of the day.

Crowley and Lodge, from *Younger Next Year*, state the value of exercise similarly. They claim, "Biologically there is no such thing as retirement, or even aging. There is only growth or decay, and your body looks to choose between them. So exercise is the master signaller, the agent that sets hundreds of chemical cascades in motion each time you get on that treadmill and sweat. It's what sets off the cycles of strengthening and repair within the muscles and the joints. It's the foundation of positive brain chemistry, and it leads to the younger life we (the authors) are promising, with its heightened immune system, its better sleep, its weight loss, insulin regulation and fat burning, its improved sexuality, its dramatic resistance to heart attack, stroke, hypertension, Alzheheimers disease, arthritis, diabetes, high cholesterol, and depression."

A critical motivator for me to exercise is a compound structure at the end of our chromosomes, called a telomere. These are small cells attached to the ends of our chromosomes. As we age, they become shorter, causing our cells to age and stop functioning properly (a.k.a. heart disease, dementia, cancer, shortened lifespan). Therefore, telomeres act as the aging clock in every cell. However, physical fitness and a healthy lifestyle can actually regrow the telomeres, making us look and feel much younger than we really are. When I exercise, I actually have a mental image of a telomere growing in length, and looking and feeling younger.

Another important chemical effect noted by Crowley and Lodge is the effect movement has on our body cytokine, or C-6 for short. This is the master chemical for inflammation (decay), and the cytokine-10, or C-10, is the master chemical for repair and growth. C-6 is produced in both the muscle cells and the bloodstream in response to exercise, and C-10 is produced in response to C-6. So one (C-6) is decay while the other (C-10) is growth. This is your body's brilliant mechanism for coupling decay and growth.

"You have 660 muscles, which make up almost 50 percent of your lean body weight," according to Crowley and Lodge. "Those 75 or 100 pounds of muscle are a massive reservoir of potential youth if you do your part. Exercise triggers repair, renewal, and growth by producing C-6. All forms of aerobic exercise produce C-6 in logarithmic proportion to both duration and intensity of exercise."

The whole idea is that inflammation controls growth, but we need to trigger enough inflammation to release growth. Thus, duration and intensity are important. Too much duration/intensity will weaken our growth as will not enough. The important thing to understand about C-10 (growth) is that it is automatically turned on by C-6. A few things to remember regarding the C-6 and C-10 relationship:

- Exercise changes your blood flow... every joint, every organ, every tiny part of your magnificent brain gets its bath of C-6, and then the wonderful rejuvenating C-10 each time you sweat.
- Only hard exercise triggers enough C-10 (growth)... when we are sedentary, the devil does indeed find work for the muscles. There is a steady slow drip of inflammation, but not enough to turn on C-10. Get enough exercise each day to sweat.
- Chronic stress produces a trickle of background C-6 (decay). C-10, however, will flood your body an hour after exercise,

releasing stress and leaving you relaxed. Exercise is a good stress because it reduces inflammation and decreases mortality.

Speaking of stress, I've mentioned in the book that stress leads to inflammation and is highly responsible for decreasing our immune system, leaving us vulnerable to disease and sickness. However, the passage above mentions needing some stress to produce growth. What is the right answer?

Actually, there are two types of stress: 1) Distress and 2) Eustress. Eustress is the stress that amps up our mind and body. It's the stress we feel when working on a deadline that motivates us. It's the healthy stress we feel when working out and producing enough inflammation to trigger growth.

Distress, on the other hand, is long periods of negative stress caused by worry and abusing our body and neurological system. In today's world, we need and should invite a certain amount of stress into our lives in an effort to grow. However, mental and physical growth comes from REST. You need to push and recover... push and recover. This is counter intuitive to today's culture in which we push to the point of exhaustion without finding an optimal balance where rest and stress work for greater efficiency.

Stress + Rest = Growth

Eustress ☺	Distress ☹
-Positive	-Generally feels unpleasant
-Energizes	-Often depletes energy
-Generally short-term	-Short-term and long-term
-Can improve performance	-Decreases performance
-Something we can handle	-Something we cannot handle

And now that the last few pages may have scared you into thinking your body is one big chemistry puzzle that can't be put back together, RELAX! Just get started and watch the amazing results and changes in your mood, behavior, and body. And if you're confused about the right level of intensity (after talking to your doctor, of course), I seriously recommend you read *Younger Next Year* because they do a wonderful job of explaining intensity. In fact, they (as do I) strongly recommend you buy a heart monitor for multiple purposes. The first of which is to measure your two natural aerobic paces, easy and hard. They both depend on two very different muscle metabolisms, which are determined by the fuel you use. Low-intensity, light aerobic exercise burns fat, while hard aerobic exercise burns glucose. Your heart rate is the only way to know for sure which metabolism is at work and what results you are getting.

Note:
In order to calculate your target heart rate: First, subtract your age from 220. If you're 60, you'll get 160. That's your theoretical MAX. Now take 60% of that... you come up with 96, which is your low end. Now calculate 70% (112), 80% (128), and 90% (144). Whatever your numbers are, memorize them; they are important. Depending on your level of fitness, you can play with these numbers somewhat, but remember your max is the pace you can maintain for only 60 seconds.

When exercising at a lower heart rate, your body is burning fat, which is where your body and brain grow. As you push the body a little harder, it starts burning glucose in addition to fat, which is stored in your muscles, and feeds it into your mitochondria (see the section on nutrition) which gives you extra energy (like a runner's high). However, as you reach your upper limits (say 80% of maximum), you burn more glucose – your high-octane gasoline equivalent. This is important because it's first necessary to build a long and sustained period of low/moderate intensity training in order to build a bigger engine that can burn the glucose, which is like running on rocket fuel.

So don't think that slow and steady is a waste of time. It takes time to build a base from which you can move into more intense aerobic, and eventually, anaerobic exercise, which is when you push your maximum heart rate up to 85% of your max. This is where you are delivering maximum oxygen and blood to your cells and kicking into a third metabolic gear. Operating in an anaerobic state is a great way to get into peak shape; however, it doesn't really do anything for longevity, or overall health… but for those training for high-level competition, it's the state they need to be in.

Probably for you and me, we can get the greatest results operating in low-medium with some high-intensity training, depending on our objectives. However, it's habit and routine that win the race. Sticking to a program of constant movement is key, as we noted from the Blue Zone. You become more fit with harder exercise, but gain more endurance and general healthiness with prolonged light exercise.

I'll end this portion on exercise by mentioning various apps and tools to monitor exercise and fitness. As you are well aware, this industry is exploding with gadgets and monitors to measure your fitness. Basic tools for heart rate and exercise goals can be found in Apple, Fitbit, or Garmin watches just to name a few. Another device for your wrist that I'm intrigued with is a wrist strap called WHOOP. This device has features similar to the Apple Watch, and measures your intensity and gives you feedback regarding peak recovery.

Exercise apps have also exploded, and there are many you can find for free on the internet (I use the Virtual Training (VT) app, which features a variety of exercises, including kettlebells, free weights, etc. at no cost). The Nike Training Club also produces a free app with plenty of variety. And, there are countless apps with membership fees that give you many of the benefits you find with a personal training coach (I've used HIIT by Daily Burn and Les Miles to name a few).

Hydration

The final portion of this chapter on physical health is hydration.

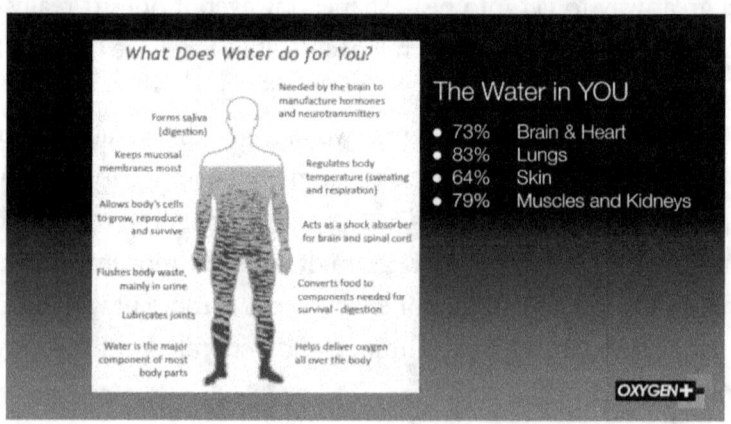

Our bodies need fluids... plain and simple. As you can see from the chart above, most of our body is made up of fluids, and when we are dehydrated, our systems shut down, and the brain begins to become fatigued. A good rule of thumb is to drink at least half an ounce of water (or non-caloric fluid) per pound that you weigh; for example, a 150-pound person should aim to drink 75-ounces per day. One of my morning rituals is to drink 8-ounces of non-chilled (warm is better) water with lemon and apple cider vinegar to kick-start my digestive system. Many world-class athletes start their mornings with lemon water since the body is dehydrated after not receiving any fluids over the past seven to nine hours. Benefits of water with lemon in the morning are:

- Good source of vitamin C
- Boost your immune system
- Supports weight loss
- Improves skin quality
- Aids in digestion
- Prevents kidney stones

And drinking water in general promotes weight loss, optimizes mood and memory, keeps the digestive system on track, and improves our fitness and exercise routines.

One caution I would like to mention is "drinking your calories." I stick to either water (lemon juice is optional) or a non-caffeinated tea (Sportea) that I buy online as you'll want to hydrate with something you enjoy but isn't adding calories or artificially stimulating the brain. Coffee (without creamer– since I don't want the calories or to break my fast when I'm intermittent fasting) is, however, a healthy stimulant with many benefits when consumed in moderation. According to the Mayo Clinic, coffee has many benefits (with dark roasted coffee having the most benefits), including a reduction in:

- Parkinson's disease
- Type 2 diabetes
- Liver disease, including liver cancer
- Heart attack and stroke

To assist in getting ample fluids throughout the day, I suggest buying that cool-looking Hydroflask in the 32 or 40-ounce size. Sipping on fluids throughout the day will keep your organs optimal, your brain fully functioning, and your joints lubricated.

Chapter 5 Key Concepts

- ☒ Sleep is absolutely essential! Sleep-related fatigue can cause diabetes/obesity, high blood pressure, heart disease, cognitive impairment, and reduced physical recovery.

- ☒ Our bodies cycle between REM (Rapid Eye Movement) and non-REM sleep. A rule of thumb is to strive for 20-25% REM of your total sleep each night. When the brain is in REM, cerebral spinal fluids wash through your brain, flushing and retaining only what you need to remember.

- ☒ Seven to eight hours of sleep is optimal for adults.

- ☒ Proteins, Carbs, and Fats (PCF) is a good guide for a healthy diet. Vegetables and fruits are essential– five (cups) is fine and nine (cups) is divine!

- ☒ Intermittent Fasting consists of three plans: 16:8, 5:2, and One Meal A Day (OMAD). Studies have found fasting to help with calorie control, increased energy from burning excess fat, as well as reduced inflammation.

- ☒ Pay close attention to your gut (a.k.a. the Second Brain). It is filled with trillions of bacteria of which some are healthy and some are not. Eat a diverse range of healthy foods (nuts, legumes, fruit with high fiber), fermented foods (yogurt and sauerkraut), and prebiotic foods (artichokes, asparagus, oats, and apples).

- ☒ A good exercise program is critical for the brain, heart, and reducing inflammation (which benefits the immune system).

- ☒ Physiological benefits of exercise are reduced cortisol (hormone of fear), and increased serotonin (happiness) and dopamine (drive). In addition, the BDNF (brain-derived neurotrophic factor) is released to repair brain cells damaged by stress.

- ☒ Fitness and movement are both aerobic (low/medium intensity, which burns fat) and anaerobic (high intensity, which burns glucose). A long and sustained aerobic exercise (60-75% of your maximum heart rate) has the same benefits (quality and quantity of life) as anaerobic exercise (80% or greater of your maximum heart rate).

- ☒ Stress+Rest=Growth

- ☒ Consume half of your body weight in ounces of non-caloric and healthy fluids each day to improve weight loss, optimize mood and memory, digestive system, and physical recovery from exercise.

CHAPTER 6

RELATIONSHIPS... A MATTER OF LIFE AND DEATH

Loneliness/Stress

Have you ever heard that someone died of a broken heart? Well, that's actually more literal than you realize. Relationships, doubts, and insecurity are a critical component to energy and longevity. In 2020, during the initial phase of the COVID-19 virus quarantine, loneliness and lack of security, along with self-isolation, created a pandemic of its own... depression.

Loneliness and stress, whether it be from a bad relationship or loss of a loved one, has a physiological effect, including hardening of the arteries (high blood pressure), inflammation (affects the immune system), diabetes, and learning and memory deficiencies. In earlier chapters, we discussed the downstream effects of stress and a poor immune system and how it accelerates disease, such as cancer and heart disease. In addition, loneliness and insecurity make us feel unsafe, both mentally and physically. As leaders, it's imperative to know and recognize not only the fallout from our personal emotional stress but also for those we lead.

In the book *The Way We're Working Isn't Working* by Tony Schwartz with Jean Gomes and Catherine McCarthy, PH.D., they punctuate the importance of our emotions as they quote Roy Baumeister, social psychologist and writer of a paper entitled, *Bad is Stronger than Good*. He states that the fear of aloneness and the absence of caring relationships are "Worse than the pain of emotional or physical abuse." As leaders, this speaks to our need to actively engage with those we work with, especially during times of stress, negative reviews, and corporate instability. Taking control and assessing our emotions and those of others is key to good leadership.

In the book *Emotional Intelligence*, author Daniel Goleman states, "You need *emotional intelligence* (EI) as it allows you to recognize and manage your feelings without being controlled by them. It fosters good social interactions because it helps put yourself in other people's shoes." It's also critical as it allows each of us to manage our thinking and emotional brain. As a leader, this is why I believe so passionately in self-awareness. The ability to understand and connect stress and loneliness to performance, chronic absenteeism and health problems is vital.

And back to our friends in the Blue Zone again, one of the nine common traits that helps centenarians live a long and lasting life is the relationships in their lives. Most of these areas in the world have strong family support systems where family generations live in the same house or close-by with an abundance of security and emotional support. For instance, the Blue Zone of Okinawa's sense of community and belonging is formalized in the system of *Moai*. Originally, this meant meeting regularly for common purposes, such as harvest or the arrangement of local festivities. Today, it's more of a ritualized vehicle for companionship. Strong community provides a purpose for the Okinawans, which also reduces stress. Sense of community is equally important in the workplace. Gallup, a global and analytics advice firm, believes a critical key to retaining happy and well-adjusted employees is "having a best friend at work." When employees possess a deep sense of affiliation, they are driven to positive actions that benefit the business, and in turn, it fuels greater individual performance. As leaders, I believe culture and community are absolutely paramount to success, and it's well documented in books like *Good to Great* by Jim Collins, *The Truth about Employee Engagement* by Patrick Lencioni, and *The Joy of Work* by Bruce Daisley.

Increasing Positive Connections Through Your "Board of Directors"

Another form of community and relationships I suggest for leaders to consider having is your own Board of Directors. A Board of Directors? For me? Only large companies form "BODs" don't they? Well, why not you? Medium and large firms pay the brightest and best to hold them accountable. They have a desire to have those with varied skills understand their business and volunteer their wisdom, experience, and knowledge to guide, direct, and elevate their business plans.

When thinking about who should be on your board, I suggest you get a variety of individuals who can assist you in all areas of your life. For example, why not have multiple directors who counsel you in the areas of faith, finance, career, health, parenting, and being the best you can be? Having three to seven individuals counsel you should be a goal in your life.

One other thing to consider is not being afraid or intimidated to approach individuals you admire because you believe that they may be too busy or operate at a different or higher level than you. Nothing could be further from the truth. In fact, most people are honored to be asked and will give up a small amount of time for a breakfast meeting, Zoom, or infrequent call. You just need to ask!

How often should I meet with my board? It depends. There are some you may wish to meet with weekly, monthly, quarterly, or bi-annually. For example, my wife and I meet with our financial advisor quarterly. We get an update on our financial situation and decide whether course correction is needed.

Renowned businessman Jim Rohn once said, "You're the average of the five people you spend most of your time with." You may not spend the majority of your time with your Board of Directors, however, getting elite advice and counsel from those you admire most will undoubtedly keep you accountable and challenged with sage advice.

Potential Board of Directors Members:

- **Faith**
  Finding someone you trust and who shares your theological values is the first step. Having someone who can keep you accountable, listens, and lives with wisdom is vital no matter your age or season of life. I mentored a young man for over 20 years as he wanted to shed demons from his past, and it's been my blessing to watch him grow as a husband, father, and business leader.

- **Financial**
  Finding a financial counselor can be tricky. Knowing your expectations and how they get paid is an important first step. You may want someone who only advises you on

financial investment or a Certified Financial Planner (CFP) who lays out a more holistic plan, including investments, insurance, retirement planning. And, while some people (very few in my opinion) can manage their investments on their own, I've always believed that investment professionals are like doctors... and I don't want to operate on myself!

- **Career/Branding/Sales Coach**
  In my experience, I've always tried to find someone who is at a senior level and whom I respect immensely. Again, don't be intimidated by their status or think they won't have the time. If they don't, they will be honest with you. But, you won't know if you don't ask. Another consideration is someone who is retired. They have experience and, in many cases, the time to sit down and discuss their life experiences. This could definitely be a "win-win" for both of you.

- **Health**
  Many health clubs offer personal trainers. Again, finding the right one can be tricky. And although this can be an expensive option, they often understand nutrition, physical fitness, and the various forms of exercise that can add flexibility, strength, and an acceptable body fat percentage. This is also an opportunity to find a certified food nutritionist, as we discussed in the previous chapter. Many grocers are now offering certified nutritionists as part of their services, too.

- **Medical/Physicians**
  Not everyone has a health plan offered through work.

However, if possible, find the absolute best doctors you can afford. This includes a general practitioner, internist, dermatologist, dentist, opthamologist, etc. Find the best specialist and make them part of your board.

- **Personal/Executive Coach**
  There are many life/executive coaches that have entered the business over the past several years. Their cost (and experience) will vary, as will their area of expertise. They would and should challenge you! Some will listen and have you draw conclusions, while some will consult and give advice. Regardless, this industry is growing and with good reason.

Is Digitalism Leading to Loneliness and Stress?

The world of digitalism is growing and now being used by all generations. As dependence on technology continues to grow, productivity and human relationships are being met with mixed results. We're digitally connected 24/7 via Facebook, Instagram, TikTok, Linkedin, and WhatApp, just to name a few. When coaching leaders, I strongly urge them to put their technology down (yes, your smart watch, phone, iPad, whatever) for one hour each day and detox.

The digital revolution was never intended by Steve Jobs or Mark Zuckerberg to create a zombie-like environment with serious health consequences. However, now, we've entered a level of 'digital obesity,' which is clearly leading to anxiety, loneliness, and sedentary lifestyles. It's a direct hit to the neurons in our brains, specifically dopamine, which can make us temporarily excited.

Professor Jerome Sarris, Deputy Director of the NICM Health Research Institute, said, "I believe that this (internet), along with the increasing #instagramification of society, has the ability to alter both the structure and functioning of the brain, while potentially also altering our social fabric."

I listened to a podcast awhile back from Cal Newport as he was launching his book *Digital Minimalism*, and he spoke on how social media is becoming the new "big tobacco." It's much more than just turning off notifications for the 132 apps you have (who needs 132 apps?). It's more about having a solid technology and social media plan that asks key questions regarding what really serves you? Is your technology really helping you make more friends? Increasing career opportunities? Making you stronger, smarter, and healthier? If so, manage it. If not, get rid of it!

And, the book isn't draconian about going cold turkey and tossing your cell phone out the window. It's about going through a digital declutter instead of a digital detox. It's about placing a call versus texting. It's about doing versus mindless consuming. Take some time and challenge yourself. And please, turn the screens off a few hours before going to bed. It's proven that limiting LED exposure is crucial for releasing melatonin and helping you fall and stay asleep.

Recognizing Stress and Loneliness

If you ever feel disconnected from others, take some solace in the fact that you're not alone. A recent study by global health service company, Cigna, found that 46% of U.S. adults report sometimes feeling lonely and 47% report feeling left out. Cigna calls those "epidemic levels." What's more, only around half of Americans say they have meaningful in-person social interactions on a daily basis, such as having an extended conversation with a friend or spending time with family members. Their study also found that loneliness affects younger Americans more than the elderly. This is only further validated from the earlier mention in this book regarding the rapid increase in enrollment at Yale University in the newly formed class, Happiness 101. As of 2019, Generation Z (usually defined as those born between 1996-2010), were the loneliest generation and Millennials (born 1980-1995) were found to be close behind.

Frustration, anxiety, and loneliness happens to all of us. As I've mentioned, the key is mitigating our chances of depression through self-diagnosis. To do this, I turn to a simple acronym called HALT, which stands for **Hungry**, **Angry**, **Lonely**, and **Tired**. This is widely used to help patients in recovery and people like you and me to identify core reasons for depression and/or low energy. We've discussed "hunger" and "tired" in Chapter 5. However, the "A" (angry) and "L" (loneliness) fit squarely into this conversation. When depressed or low on energy, HALT is a good indicator that I'm not eating well, something has set me off, I've been sequestered from human or social situations way too long, and/or I'm just plain tired. And while the awareness and ability to diagnose any of these traits doesn't guarantee immediate success, it will give you solace and grace that "this too shall pass" if you just make some adjustments in an effort to get back on track.

And while loneliness and anger can lead to depression, other situations outside of our control, like losing a loved one or loss of purpose (a job) greatly enhance the physiological effects mentioned earlier (hardened arteries, diabetes, inflammation, loss of short term memory, etc.). Everything in this book ties together self-awareness, understanding how you react under stress, getting the appropriate sleep, eating the right foods, and having a reason to wake up in the morning. Happiness and contentment are well within our reach if we just apply ourselves to these basic concepts.

A quote that I often refer to is "The key to happiness is something to look forward to, something to do, and someone to love." Yes, relationships are just as key to our longevity as a great work out, healthy meal, or a great night's sleep. So unplug from the digital world and plug into family, friends, co-workers, and all of the interesting people that make up this wonderful world. It's a matter of life and death!

Chapter 6 Key Concepts

- ☒ Loneliness and stress have physiological effects on the body, leading to hardening of the arteries (high blood pressure), inflammation (affects the immune system), diabetes, and learning and memory deficiencies.

- ☒ Strong family and community relationships are a key element in each of the five Blue Zone communities around the world.

- ☒ Create your own "Board of Directors" for both counsel and mentoring relationships. Having a well-rounded board should consist of someone(s) in the areas of career, financial advising, doctors, faith/accountability, health, a skill you want to improve, executive/life coach, etc.

- ☒ Digital obesity is becoming a pandemic. The internet and cell phones are great devices as long as we manage them (vs. the other way around).

- ☒ Surfing the internet causes a spike in the neuron dopamine, which gives us gratification.

- ☒ This gratification is short term and addicting. Social media and digital developers are well aware of how your brain works and their ability to guide your decisions.

- ☒ While loneliness affects everyone, Gen Z and Millenials are far more affected than other generations.

- ☒ Some degree of human and personal interaction is key for everyone's emotional energy and overall health.

- ☒ Hunger, Anger, Loneliness, and Tired (HALT) is a wonderful acronym for self-diagnosis when energy levels are low and/or depressed.

CHAPTER 7

THE ZEN SIDE OF LIFE

I've really become a student of neuroscience and the wonderful ways that we can "train the brain," or as some say, "fire and wire," through activities such as meditation, journaling, and visualization. As a recovering "monkey brain" who has a harder time with focus and execution than most, I've found this area to be absolutely intriguing and beneficial in re-shaping my life.

A fancy neuroscience word to remember is neuroplasticity. This is the ability for the brain to grow, reorganize synaptic connections, especially in response to learning, experience, or following injury. And while this is really beneficial for those recovering from a stroke or overcoming dyslexia, it's super cool for you and me to know that our brains don't quit growing... even as we age. We just need to keep exercising the brain as we would a muscle. And for me, every morning kicks off bright and early, firing and the wiring, getting the rest of the day jump started and headed the right direction.

Chapter 7

Mindful Living

"I can't meditate… my mind keeps wandering… I don't know the right way to meditate… how long should I meditate and when?" These are the common replies when I ask whether a leader is giving attention to mindfulness in order to get quality "me time" in an effort to relax, focus, and find an inner-calm. Meditation is a key practice to living a mindful life. And, meditation is really nothing more than letting the brain slow down through breathing techniques two to three times each day in order to get clarity and mental rest.

The "monkey brain" I mentioned earlier is a phrase Buddhists use in reference to endless chattering and scrambling about for no discernible purpose. Only today, the monkey is all wired up on technology and drugs. To that point, according to an article in the New York Times, more than 30 million Americans are currently taking anti-depressant drugs. Middle-aged women seem to be most susceptible, with a rate of one out of four women in their 40s and 50s on an anti-depressant. And as mentioned in the earlier chapter, computers and digital technologies have placed an overabundance of distracting devices in our hands.

While meditation is like any other muscle that needs time to develop, I really urge you to make it a part of your daily routine (more about routines in Chapter 10). I typically spend 15-20 minutes each morning clearing the mind, visualizing, and incorporating prayer and gratitude into my practice.

So what is the right way to practice meditation? The Buddhists are said to have taught 84,000 ways to attain enlightenment. Eighty-four thousand!! And that's just the Buddhists. So finding "your" way to meditate is essential and may take some time. There are many guided meditation apps that will lead your meditation practice effectively. HeadSpace, Calm, Simple Mind, and Mindless Training App are popular, just to name a few. I use Calm and Simple Mind, as I enjoy the training along with the many options it provides regarding the sessions aimed at morning, midday or evening. In addition, they provide specific meditations for specific struggles or music conducive to various moods. I also coach leaders on visualization techniques that will be discussed later in this chapter.

However, if you're just starting out, I suggest picking a quiet place and a set time(s) during the day and use a timer (I use my Apple watch) so that you don't have to worry about when to stop. You can start by either sitting still in a chair or sitting on a pillow (the bare ground is just too uncomfortable) that keeps the spine straight. Meditation is really just a way to focus, empty the brain, and become mindless as a method to find mental neutrality and allow the body to restore. Finding a breathing technique or "one thing" to focus on is critical. My mind tends to wander during my practice, and I've come to realize that's exactly why we meditate. It's to train our cerebral muscles to continuously reign in our thoughts and learn to focus. Whether you learn multiple breathing techniques or the ability to focus on a thought, an object, or an emotion, the key is to dial everything back and learn to focus... on nothing!

Breathing techniques

Breathing techniques associated with meditation is a science in and of itself. Breathing techniques will instantly calm the mind and the body, giving you a feeling of equanimity. Box breathing is very popular and is one I use daily. Box breathing is basically breathing in and out through the nose slowly and methodically with periods of holding your breath. The method is to breathe through the nose for the count of five, hold for the count of five, breathe out through the nose for the count of five and hold for the count of five. This technique can lower blood pressure and provide an almost immediate sense of calm. The slow holding of breath allows CO_2 to build up in the blood. An increased blood CO_2 level stimulates the parasympathetic nervous system, which relaxes the mind and body.

Another technique is nostril breathing also known as Nadi Shodhana. Air inhaled through the left nostril triggers the rest/relaxation response (parasympathetic nervous system) and inhaling through the right stimulates the fight/flight response (sympathetic nervous system). To do this effectively, you use your thumb and ring finger. If you're right handed, use your thumb to close your right nostril while breathing in deeply through your left nostril. Then, exhale through your left nostril. Alternate nostrils by using your ring finger to close your left nostril and inhale, and exhale deeply through your right nostril. The benefits of this practice can calm or energize the body depending on how you regulate the depth, length, and energy of the breath. Five key benefits are 1) Revitalization, 2) Enhanced Mental Function, 3) Calmness and Better Sleep, 4) Soothed Nervous System, and 5) Regulated Body Temperature.

A final method I often use is concentrating on a state of mindlessness or neutrality, focusing on neither positive nor negative thoughts and training the mind to stay in this state for as long as possible. When I drift, I acknowledge it and come back as often as possible. I find this helps me with disciplined focus throughout the day and helps me draw back to centered focus.

Yoga

Another way to meditate, exercise and center the mind is Yoga. *Yoga Journal Magazine* listed 38 health benefits from yoga, including blood pressure regulation, improving blood sugar and cholesterol levels, boosting the immune system, improving balance, maintaining the nervous system, and strengthening the spine to relieve pain. Yoga can also improve digestion, optimize sleep, and combat depression.

I practice Yoga at least twice a week using a paid app called Yoga Studio: Mind & Body. While there are numerous yoga apps to choose from, if you don't mind paying $70 annually, this one is fantastic! Not only does it have multiple yoga classes for beginner, intermediate, and advanced, but it also specializes in meditation classes, family yoga, yoga for mental health, yoga for the immune system, and MANY more. These classes are also customized for 10, 15, 30, and 60 minutes, which makes it really convenient to fit into your schedule.

Brain Waves

So what really goes on in the brain while we're meditating? There's actually a lot of electrical energy being generated when the brain's neurons communicate with one another. Just like sound or light, the energy created in the brain waves can be measured in frequency (wave cycles per second) and are quantified by a unit known as hertz (Hz), which have a frequency of one cycle per second = 1 Hz. The five brain waves (six if you count the infra-low wave that is essential to brain timing and network function) are:

Delta waves (.5 to 3 Hz), which are generated in deepest meditation and dreamless sleep. These waves suspend external awareness and are the source of empathy, healing, and regeneration. This is why deep sleep is so critical to the healing process.

Theta waves (3 to 8 Hz) are mostly found in sleep and/or deep meditation. Theta is critical for learning, memory, and intuition. This is more of our dream state and is where we hold our "stuff," like fears, troubled history, and nightmares.

Alpha waves (8 to 12 Hz) are the resting state for the brain, which is dominant during quietly flowing thoughts and some meditation. This is a great state for overall mental coordination, alertness, mind/body integration, and learning.

Beta waves (12 TO 38 Hz) dominate our normal waking state where attention is directed towards cognitive tasks and the outside world. The beta waves are broken into three different bands as they go through the stages of a "fast idle" when we are musing, a high engagement when we are figuring something out, and highly complex thought as we are integrating new experiences.

Gamma waves (38 TO 42 Hz) are the fastest frequency and often found when we are processing from different brain areas. Gamma brainwaves pass information rapidly and quietly. And while this state is the most subtle of the frequencies, the mind has to be quiet to access gamma.

So what does all of this mean as it relates to yoga, meditation, and quieting the mind? When our brain waves are out of balance, there will be corresponding problems in our emotional or neuro-physical health. Over-arousal in certain brain areas is linked to anxiety disorders, sleep problems, nightmares, behavior, anger/aggression, and agitated depression. However, by altering our brainwaves and quieting the mind with meditation and yoga (as opposed to chemical substances, such as medication or recreational drugs), it's possible to alter your brainwave state and train or fine tune your brain waves to balance. Being in the alpha state (clear headed, present, and fully in the moment) vs. the beta state (where we spend most of our days on mental overload) is CRITICAL. We can get into the alpha state in several ways:

- Drinking tea (black, green, or white), which contains Theanine, which is known to generate alpha brain waves
- Aerobic exercise (about 30-40 minutes of exercise and/or yoga) is a great way to kick in the alpha state.
- Being in nature and just walking, sitting, and admiring God's creation
- A glass of wine (but don't overdo it!) can slow down the brain waves
- Positive/uplifting music (I listen to jazz and piano classics on Spotify, or famous movie scores)
- Meditation/breathing techniques are probably the best, however. The ability to quiet the mind with a daily routine is a great way to get in the alpha state and prepare for beta!

Training the brain to relax and not hit the panic button can reduce the genes that produce inflammation, which is how the body deals with stress and pain. As mentioned in previous chapters, stress has a major influence on our lymphatic system, which is directly related to numerous health related issues, including various diseases. Being conscious of getting into the alpha state several times throughout the day is a great way to live with intention and a sense of calm. One suggestion is to actively schedule in your calendar specific blocks of time to stop, meditate, and get into the alpha state. I typically pick a time early in the morning and late in the evening. Anything in between is icing on the cake! And if meditating just doesn't seem to work, laughter has also been scientifically proven to have many of the same benefits including presence, lightness, connection, stress reduction, and emotional release.

Visualization

The art of visualization is tricky, yet a game changer for athletes and those wanting to improve performance. The practice has been around forever, and the only magic to the practice is how the brain functions as a way of "seeing it first." The best reference my wife and I ran across is the book *Psycho Cybernetics* by Maxwell Maltz. Maltz was a plastic surgeon who realized that while people can change self image from the outside in, it isn't until you change from the inside out that deep, long lasting change can occur. I recently spoke at an event where a very accomplished athlete approached me afterwards to tell me that his college baseball coach wouldn't issue uniforms until every player had read *Psycho Cybernetics*. The book has sold over 35 million copies over the last 35 years and continues to be one of the best self-help books in the industry.

The brain plays such a unique and complex part in performance training, yet the ability to visualize is a muscle that needs lots of work in order to get the results you want. You see, the brain actually moves toward a mentally conceived target once it has been envisioned in the brain. To go further, your physical brain and nervous system make up a servo-mechanism, goal-seeking device that operates automatically like a self-aimed torpedo or missile. The process of "steering the brain" is called "cybernetics," which comes from a Greek word literally meaning "steersman." When Maxwell looked at the human brain and its ability to steer towards results (cybernetics), he coined the term psycho cybernetics. Psycho cybernetics acts as a heat-seeking missile or torpedo as we move towards our goals by going forward, making errors, and continually correcting our course.

The power and the role the brain plays is so unbelievably complex that British neurophysicist W. Grey Walter said that at least ten billion electronic cells would be needed to build a facsimile of man's brain. These cells would occupy about a million and a half cubic feet, and several additional millions of cubic feet would be needed for the "nerves" and wiring. Power to operate it would be one billion watts. That's incredible and something only God can manufacture, in my realm of thinking. As humans, we have barely tapped into the potential of rewiring our brains and working that muscle differently toward a desired goal or result. You must trust the process and not be afraid of lack of results in the beginning. The trust process is necessary because your creative mechanisms operate below the level of consciousness and work magically over time with the repetitive acts of seeing the end result and visualization.

Psycho cybernetics stems from using our imagination, and imagination is the key to visualization as long as you keep your imagination healthy and positive. It's often said "we fear more in our imagination than we do our reality." Our brains are mostly wired to jump to imagining the worst outcome, and we spend all day playing those feelings out. However, using our imagination constructively every day allows us to act, feel, and become the person God intended us to be from the start! Your nervous system cannot tell the difference between an imagined experience or a real experience. It reacts automatically to information that you give to it based on what you think or imagine to be true.

So utilizing the act of visualization, or "role playing," is the genesis of creating a positive, goal-driven outcome that allows the nerves to relax because, basically, the script has already been written, and now it's time to go from rehearsal to the live stage. The rehearsal (visualization) process is played out like a movie role, and you are the star. The ability to quiet the mind and sense every detail of the various scenes, including the smells, the background chatter, and every nuance related to the story is key.

We've all read stories of famous athletes who had played the game or round before it ever started. Ben Hogan, the great golfer, for example, was so keen on mentally rehearsing before every shot that all he had to do was step up and let muscle-memory take over just as he imagined. While I was introduced to visualization and relaxation techniques in high school, one of my biggest regrets is not making this a core component of every facet of my life from that day forward. Please don't misunderstand the need for hard work, it's just that mentally seeing and visualizing goes hand in hand with the work needed to prepare for an interview, play a golf match, seek that promotion, or whatever life changing goals you want to master.

There are several ways to use visualization, one of which I mentioned is playing the lead role in your made-for-success movie. Another key method, according to Dr. Harry Emerson Fosdick is to, "Hold a picture of yourself long and steadily enough in your mind's eye, and you will be drawn towards it." Never visualize the negative, only see the positive, and picture it vividly as great living starts with a picture that is held in your imagination, letting cybernetics take over.

Set aside a period of 30 minutes each day (yes, that's a lot of time) in a relaxed and comfortable position. While 30 minutes is a long time, I typically tack on 15 minutes of visualization to my normal ten minutes of meditation, as that allows me to set the stage for a more effective experience. Again, pay attention to small details when visualizing– noticing sights, sounds, smells, etc. If the imagination is vivid enough, the practice will be equivalent to an actual experience insofar as the nervous system is concerned. Try to play the role as you see yourself already, having the confidence you desire. See and feel the experience of being in control and letting the experience play out on your terms versus forcing the situation.

Another book I often reference when speaking is *Executive Toughness* by Jason Selk. Selk was the Director of Mental Training for the St. Louis Cardinals and is a top-tier executive coach and expert on teaching people how to develop mental toughness. One key takeaway Selk took from his time working with professional athletes was that of breathing and visualization. His key techniques before and during competition were the ability to breath in deeply for six seconds, hold for two seconds, and exhale for seven seconds, and after the breathing, create an identity statement or personal mantra of who you are and who you want to be. For example, "*I outwork the competition everyday, and I am the most effective performance coach and sought-after speaker in the country. I experience true love as a husband and father.*"

In addition, create a personal highlight reel. Decide in detail who you want to be and how you want your life to be in approximately five years. Spend 30 seconds visualizing yourself as this person. For another 30 seconds, visualize those things you need to do in the upcoming days to be moving toward your *who* and *how* for your life. Then repeat your identity statement and finish with the breathing exercise you started with.

When it comes to visualization, you need to find what works for you. I have a day planner with my goals and visions for my life that I look at first thing EVERY morning. I then use those goals and visions as part of my meditation and visualization visualizing myself as an accomplished author and a nationally recognized keynote speaker working with dozens of executives and their teams around the world. I envision the work it will take to accomplish this, along with the feeling and sensation I get from seeing leaders grow and having gratitude for a better life. These techniques, whether event oriented (i.e., athletics or a work situation) or just desiring a better and more positive life really will work as long as you create the daily routine (which we will cover in Chapter 10) and trust the experience.

Journaling

Journaling is a lost art that's making a robust comeback! The art of brain-dumping everything into a notebook, whether it be early in the day or before bedtime, is scientifically proven to release toxic emotions and free up the brain for maximum creativity! Just the ability to get tangled thoughts and frustrations on paper or to simply list what we're grateful for increases the dopamine and serotonin in our brain waves, leaving us calm and with better clarity to tackle the day or start a good night's sleep.

Other reasons to journal are noted below in an article in the *Daily Stoic*, called "The Art of Journaling: How to Start Journaling, Benefits of Journaling, and More:"

- According to a study conducted by Harvard Business School, participants who journaled at the end of the day had a 25% increase in performance when compared with a control group who did not journal. As the researchers conclude, "Our results reveal reflection to be a powerful mechanism behind learning, confirming the words of American philosopher, psychologist, and educational reformer John Dewey: 'We do not learn from experience… we learn from reflecting on experience.'"
- Another Study by Cambridge University found journaling helps improve well-being after traumatic and stressful events. Participants asked to write about such events for 15–20 minutes resulted in improvements in both physical and psychological health.
- Improved Communication Skills – A Stanford University study found the critical relationship between writing and speaking. Writing reflects clear thinking, and in turn, clear communication.
- A study by *The Journal of Social and Personal Relationships* found that writing "focused on positive outcomes in negative situations" decreases emotional distress.
- Improved Sleep – *The Journal of Experimental Psychology* found that journaling before bed decreases cognitive stimulus, rumination, and worry, allowing you to fall asleep faster.
- Boosted Cognition – Research published to *The Journal of Experimental Psychology* found that reflective writing reduces intrusive and avoidant thoughts about negative events and improves working memory. These

improvements, in turn, free up our cognitive resources for other mental activities, including our ability to cope more effectively with stress.

The key to journaling is to just write. And I mention writing versus typing for a reason. Science is now telling us that the art of writing develops a stronger conceptual understanding than typing. Handwriting forces your brain to mentally engage with the information, improving both literacy and memory retention. However, don't let your desire to type (vs. writing) stop you from journaling. Writing with a pen is just a way to slow down your brain, your thoughts, and take the necessary time to process.

And, if you are inclined to begin writing, I strongly urge you to buy Pilot FriXion pens, which are erasable. This was a game changer to encourage me to write more. They glide as easy as any ballpoint pen and erase with ease. This allows me to write freely knowing that I can erase when the hand gets ahead of the brain. In addition to writing with a pen, the Apple pencil is a great way to write, doodle, and be creative with your thoughts on devices such as an iPad. I use the Apple pencil (along with the FriXion pens) daily, and I'll touch more on this in a later chapter as we discuss routines.

As I begin to journal, whether it be morning or evening, I typically brain dump. I just start spewing anything that's weighing heavily on my mind. I try to get issues on paper, out of the head, create awareness, and just have a place to park them. Journaling, however, has many benefits in addition to clarity and awareness. It's a great way to list what you're grateful for (see dopamine/serotonin hit). It helps you organize the day ahead or list wins and learning moments before you go to bed. It can capture life experiences and be a reflection of where your mind and attitude were during the past month. I always go back and read the past 2-3 weeks of my journaling, and it always amazes me that the problems or anxiety I wrote about are already ancient history. The axiom of "this too shall pass" becomes extremely evident knowing that nothing is permanent. And just to kick start my journaling on most mornings, I have a checklist on the first page of my Moleskin journal with these topics:

- What adversity should I be running toward in order to grow?
- Who or what (in addition to my family and friends) am I grateful for?
- Who has been coming to my mind, and when specifically will I reach out to them?
- What am I NOT doing that would grow my business, career, or relationships 2X?
- How is my energy (physical, emotional, mental, and purpose)? What areas are "on fire" and which ones need attention?
- Lately, I've found myself to be at my absolute best when...
- Today would be awesome if I focused on...
- The best way to approach _____ is to...

As mentioned, these are just kick starter topics. There is NO WRONG WAY TO JOURNAL! Don't worry about how long you should journal or what time of day. Write from the heart, and don't be afraid to let some heavy stuff out. History is littered with great leaders who journaled daily, including Thomas Jefferson, Benjamin Franklin, Mark Twain, Ronald Reagan, Napoleon, Marcus Aurelius (and all Stoics for that matter), and Martina Naratilova, just to name a few; and, their style and purpose for writing varied greatly.

However, they all had one thing in common, a constant practice or ritual aimed at getting something on paper (or computer) for a purpose that benefitted them personally.

I mentioned that I use a plain notebook (specifically, a Moleskin because of the quality of paper); however, there are many products on the market that are great for guiding your journaling experience. I've used *The Five Minute Journal* and enjoyed it. The *Daily Stoic Journal* is also a great resource, as is *The One Line a Day Journal*.

Chapter 7 Key Concepts

- ☒ When our brain waves are out of balance, there will be corresponding problems in our emotional or neurophysical health. Overarousal in certain brain areas is linked to anxiety disorders, sleep problems, nightmares, behavior issues, anger, aggression, and agitated depression.

- ☒ It's possible to alter our brainwaves and quiet the mind with meditation and yoga (as opposed to medication or recreational drugs) in an effort to train/fine tune/balance the brainwaves.

- ☒ Of all brainwaves, the alpha state is optimal. This is the resting state for the brain, which is dominant during quietly flowing thoughts and some meditation. This is a great state for overall mental coordination, alertness, mind/body integration and learning.

- ☒ Visualization or "role playing" is the genesis of creating a positive, goal-driven outcome that allows the nerves to relax because basically the script has already been written, and now it's time to go from rehearsal/practice to the live stage.

- The brain actually moves towards a mentally conceived target (servo-mechanism) once it has been envisioned in the brain.

- Journaling is the art of brain-dumping everything into a notebook whether it be early in the day or before bedtime. It is scientifically proven to release toxic emotions, freeing up the brain for maximum creativity!

LIVING WITH INTENTION

CHAPTER 8

SIMPLIFYING OUR STUFF AND OUR EXPERIENCES

We live in the land of plenty, and as Americans, we control over 30% of the world's wealth, yet, we're not exactly the happiest campers. And while I understand that income inequality exists, chances are that most of those reading this book are employable, have food to eat and have adequate shelter. We work hard, stress or covet what we don't have, fearing the future and living to a ripe old age... yet, having never really LIVED!

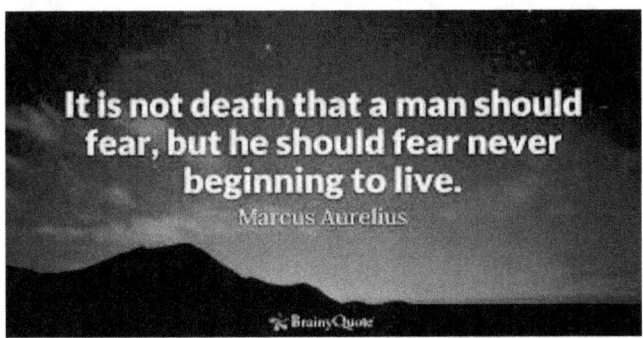

It is not death that a man should fear, but he should fear never beginning to live.
Marcus Aurelius

As most people start to grow older, the sense of moving from success to significance starts to settle in. Now, I don't want to generalize the younger generations (namely Millennials and Gen Z), but I really think they have it right! They're challenging the status quo that older generations have latched onto and are not as worried about the future unless it pertains to environmental sustainability or happiness. And while many in the older generations have created safety nets of financial gains to pass down, I still sense that essentialism and security would still be their lifestyle of choice.

Spend your money on Experiences... Not Stuff

A story I often tell when speaking is that of the most FANTASTIC trip I ever imagined! And it took place with nothing more than moving my daughter from Milwaukee to Phoenix. To set the story and give it proper context with the message above, my daughter and son-in-law both had come to the realization at a young age that aspirations towards having the perfect house and 2.4 children and living everyone else's dream just wasn't going to cut it. And after having to endure a heartbreaking and devastating loss of our daughter's best friend and maid of honor to a senseless and tragic event, this only endorsed their idea to explore life and live to the fullest.

Life is full of very unexplainable events that should never happen! But they do. And when they do, it makes everyone of us stop and take stock in what's important and reminds us all of the lack of guarantees we have on planet earth.

On their drive home from the funeral in Iowa back to Milwaukee, Wisconsin, my daughter, Kadi and her husband, Eric, decided life was too short to not live exactly as they wanted to, which to them, included living in the Southwest. So, two months later, Eric moved to Phoenix to get a jump-start on his job search, get established, and find a home. After a few months and successfully finding work, it was Kadi's turn to make the move from Milwaukee to the desert. So she called and asked if I could take some time from work and make the 22-hour trip with her. As a dad (and if you're not, this may not resonate), you jump at the chance to spend isolated time with your children at any cost. But here's where the generational gap and story supports my theory that the younger generation "gets it."

As I graciously said that I could swing the time away from work, I went into dad mode— plugging in the miles, hours, and most efficient way of getting across Iowa, Nebraska, Colorado, New Mexico, and finally to Phoenix. With sheer precision, I thought I nailed it by mapping out the drive, sharing duties, and efficiently making this 22-hour trip in only one and a half days... as long as we took off at 8 AM sharp and kept restroom breaks to a minimum.

Upon calling her back with this glorious news from my research, she calmly and politely said, "That sounds interesting, but I did some calculations of my own."

Huh?

"You see, Dad, if we take our time, enjoy the scenery and several stops along the way, I figure we can make it in three or four days at most."

Oh crap! This is where the student teaches the master. This is the time in which you look at yourself and say "Who really gets it here?"

I gladly adopted her plan of attack, and we took off... at some non-exact time during the day. We had said goodbye to my wife, who was a secretary at an elementary school at the time and didn't have the luxury of a flexible schedule. So Kadi and I took off in her old crossover SUV— with bad tires and more miles on it than made sense. We were crammed into this car better than most Formula One drivers in their single seat cockpits readying themselves for the 24 hours of Le Mans.

My daughter's sense and skill of photography made the need to stop and take in the beauty along the way only that much better. The first experience along the way was one that I was able to give her. While I don't want to offend my friends from Nebraska, is there really that much to write home about as you go through the flattest land on God's earth (other than the Bonneville Salt Flats in Utah)? And while the scenery may not change for several hours, this state does host some unique food that I've had the opportunity to experience.

So, I led off with asking her if she had ever experienced Runza? Now this may not be everyone's favorite sandwich, and you probably won't find it in the previous chapter regarding "healthy nutrition," but this Swiss mushroom burger consisting of beef, cabbage/sauerkraut, onions, and seasoning packed into a yeast bread pocket "ain't bad!"

That meal got us through the flat lands of Nebraska until we came upon a nasty storm. However, to Kadi, the storm made the skies unique and worthy of a roadside stop. This was a great photo op of nothing but cool skies and a chance to enjoy Nebraska and the beautiful terrain I had not noticed in my past.

After having made it to Denver for a good night's sleep, the next morning we found our way to Colorado Springs. Because of my travels over the years at work, I know for a fact this is a gem of an area with things such as Pikes Peak and a wonderful and unique culture to explore on a Saturday morning. And as luck would have it, it was family weekend at the Air Force football game, of which we stopped to take in the sites and do a little hiking close by. From there, we spent some time touring downtown and embracing wonderful foods (which will still not be found in the nutrition section of this book) and exploring all that Colorado Springs has to offer.

From this point we continued to make good time heading "directionally" towards Arizona, preferring to take back roads versus highways. I've travelled for business more than most people, but I've never stopped and explored so many places along the way. We took in the wonderful sites in Taos, New Mexico, which I had heard about but never thought to spend quality time. We drove through elevations of 7,000 feet, through a beautiful area called Eagle Nest in Ute Park (another place I never knew existed!). We finished off the evening in terrain that my daughter was more familiar with: Albuquerque. She and her husband, Eric, had lived in Albuquerque, New Mexico, a couple of years earlier while he was in grad school. Again, we had a wonderful dinner at her recommendation (El Pinto, which is FANTASTIC) and breakfast the next morning at one of my favorites (Wecks, which is one of the few places that can fill my appetite), and stopped by to grab a Golden Pride breakfast burrito on the way out of town.

As we left Albuquerque, we again took the back roads, exploring the reservations of New Mexico before entering Arizona, where the weather got cooler (huh?). Again, having flown in and out of Phoenix countless times on business, I never knew just two hours from Phoenix could have elevations of 7,000 feet and be 20-30 degrees cooler. We drove through the small, beautiful town of Payson, and then descended into the "valley" of Phoenix, which was rich with scenery.

We arrived in our Formula One-style packed car well fed, and while our backsides were a little sore from the drive, the richness of our conversations and time along the way was priceless. I needed to

Chapter 8

spend a few days in Phoenix on business anyway, so it was nice to know that the trip back would be much quicker.

A few days later, I said my good byes and wished them well on their new ventures. I boarded the plane and, fortunately, sat in the window seat. The plane thrusted and took off into a cloudless sky on its way back to Des Moines. As the plane flew over virtually the same route we had just spent three days driving, it gave me a chance to look at the mountains below differently. It made me realize I couldn't see the small towns and beauty that we had witnessed just days earlier. The time passed and work started to creep back into my mind again as the plane flew over Nebraska, getting closer to home. The plane landed and touched down in just a little over three hours after takeoff.

I grabbed my bags and was walking through the airport when I had the notion to stop and text my daughter. My message was simple. It stated it took us three long days to drive, endlessly at times, in an effort to make it to Arizona. Yet, it took only three short hours for me to fly back to Iowa.

What a waste of time that flight was!

The reason I went into such detail on this story is not for you to relive a story that is probably more special to my daughter and me. It's that we all want to experience life. However, money, time, and other things always become deterrents, and bundling small, unexpected experiences can bring us just as rich and intentional life experiences as expensive and well-thought out vacations.

I mentioned in an earlier chapter that happiness is someone to love, something to look forward to, and something to do. This aspect of something to look forward to is critical for all leaders as we go through life. The ability to unplug, rest, and take on as many experiences as possible is just as important and relevant to your professional success as your personal life. The importance of "play" and rest from daily work and stress is critical to developing solutions and rebooting the hard drive (brain).

I listened to Duncan Wardle, former Head of Innovation and Creativity at Disney speak last year, and he asked an interesting question, "Where do you come up with your best ideas?" He gave everyone a minute to think about their answer. He then spoke and said, "Did anyone list their office (place of work) as an answer?"

Silence... then laughter! Of course it's in the shower, on the golf course, running, exercising, or anywhere that's not work. Scheduling your "down time" or "margin" is a CRITICAL step for everyone, especially leaders. I personally use the Michael Hyatt Planner to list my goals, chunk them into manageable pieces, and plan each quarter/month/week/day with weekly assessments of my successes/obstacles. Within this system, I plan my experiences and margin away from work, whether it's a three-day weekend or a major trip I need to plan for a year out.

At the time of this writing, I've planned several three-day weekends to finish writing this book, as well as two trips next year, one to walk portions of the Camino Santiago in Portugal/Spain with two friends and another to Dublin, Ireland with my wife. Only 28% of Americans plan to max out their vacation days, according to CNBC.com, while other studies show just 50% taking their allotted time away from the office.

We've all read the stories regarding those who take their work with them on these vacations, and I'll be the first to admit, my system is to not totally unplug. I take my laptop, but only look at it every 48-72 hours and for just one hour. My goal is to delete the noise and quickly assess if any major fires are burning (and while that is relative, it's never anything that can't wait), and it allows me to be relatively relaxed upon my return, knowing that I can catch up in a day or so versus an entire week. If you can unplug totally, that's healthier! If you feel the need to look at your work daily, you may have a work situation that isn't healthy in the first place, and I would love to talk about that in a future coaching session!

Essentialism

I prefer to use the word essentialism instead of minimalism since I, personally, can't wrap my head around having only two t-shirts, one pair of pants, two pairs of shoes, a tooth brush and limited furniture to watch the television I can't have. However, I do believe that the majority of us are blessed and lived in a world where we have clothes/possessions that we haven't used in six months (or probably more), vehicles that stretch our monthly budget, and personal possessions that really aren't relevant or needed as time passes by.

Don't get me wrong, as a guy who is blessed to have two homes in different climates, I struggle with essentialism as much as anyone. However, as a very practical person (i.e., our vehicles are nice but have well over 100,000 miles on them), if our possessions were the reason we couldn't take advantage of life's experiences, it would be time to re-evaluate our lifestyle. And the key reason I try to practice essentialism is twofold.

First, it's an injustice to God, who blessed us with possessions that I haven't used in six months, knowing that we can donate or sell to someone who really appreciates our excess.

Secondly, it frees the mind to live with less. The lack of clutter, the ease of knowing what you possess and where it's located frees the brain from negative energy, clearing it for issues that really matter. It's a detox from possessions and the realization that we really only use 30-40% of what we own.

And like the practice of planning for margin in our life, essentialism takes equal planning and effort. It involves writing in your planner, specific weeks or times each quarter or sometime during the year to simplify, organize, and gain clarity by essentializing every area of your life. Part of essentialism is purchasing items, tools, or applications to simplify. My prized possession is my Eagle Creek bag for my backpack that organizes my technology chords/plugs/etc., and it keeps only what's regularly used and essential.

Notice the areas in your life where energy could be greater if you had less and, in turn, felt more clarity and focus in your life. Those are the areas to focus on first, and by continuing the practice throughout the year, you'll see that it's an ongoing practice that yields energy and freedom.

Speaking of technology, while going "paperless" seems hard to do in today's world, scanning apps have come a long way in an effort to scan, file, and keep your information close. Personally, I use Scanner Pro, and the quality of the pictures and ability to file folders is only getting better. I scan everything from bills, insurance policies, wills/trust, titles/licenses, and just about anything. I also use a password app (1Password, RoboForm, DASHLANE, NordPass, just to name a few) to keep the hundreds of passwords, account numbers, financial data at my fingertips versus scribbled on various Post-It notes, and it also allows me to have multiple passwords to better secure our accounts. Technology is here to stay, and as mentioned in earlier chapters, it can be our friend or our enemy. This is an area where technology can simplify and make our life easier.

A good book to read is *Essentialism* by Greg McKeown. In this book, the author lists four key areas of essentialism, but not all are related to possessions:

- *Do less, but do it better.* The cornerstone of essentialism is the never-ending task of identifying the less important things in your life that you need to cut out, and doing what's left over to a higher standard. (Note: see the quote in Chapter 1 regarding saying "no" to the things that don't matter so that you can say "yes" to the things that are important).

- *Reject the notion that we should accomplish everything,* and instead, choose specific directions in which you can excel. Essentialism isn't about making tiny amounts of progress in many directions. Instead, choose a direction and make great strides in the things that matter most to you.

- *Constantly question yourself, and update your plans accordingly.* The process of deciding what's worth doing and what should be let go of is ongoing. The essentialist is always deciding whether what she is doing is actually worth her time or if she should invest her time and energy in more productive areas.

- Finally, once those few vital tasks have been distilled from the trivial many, the essentialist wastes no time ensuring the changes are put in place.

Essentialism is really about embracing the idea of "less but better" and accepting trade-offs as an inherent part of life. Optimizing our time, possessions, and decisions, declutters our brain—freeing up energy, money, and choices at work and home.

"If one's life is simple, contentment has to come. Simplicity is extremely important for happiness" - Dalai Lama

Chapter 8 Key Concepts

- ☒ Spend money on experiences... not stuff.
- ☒ Experiences and memories come in all shapes and sizes. Never pass up the small opportunities.
- ☒ Plan your margin and downtime in your planner or calendar months in advance. Whether it be three day weekends or 7-10 days of total unplugging, it's essential to your creativity and problem solving.
- ☒ Essentialism is the idea that "less is better." Essentialism can be possessions, time, and/or decisions to declutter the mind freeing up time and energy to focus on what you do best.
- ☒ Schedule day(s) throughout the year or each quarter to consistently purge and organize all areas of your life. This includes home, work, and files on your laptop/computer.

CHAPTER 9

IT'S EASIER TO GET A GOOD BRAND... THAN IT IS TO LOSE A BAD ONE

Personal branding isn't something we think about nearly enough. From the time we wake up until the time we retire each night, our brand is on display. We brand ourselves externally by the clothes we wear, the things we say, and the choices we make. Everyone from co-workers, family, friends, and general acquaintances are forming opinions based on the brand we convey. What are they really seeing though? Are they seeing our inner selves or just those attributes above the surface that allow us to look artificially good?

Why is your brand important and why should we care what others think or feel? Is it important that others know the "real" you? I once took a 360° leadership assessment with various comments at the end of the survey. A lot of the comments were positive and affirming. However, some of the comments made me reflect and feel frustrated and feel as though they really didn't know me. The coach for this exercise, however, made a profound statement, leaving me to think differently. She merely said, "Perception becomes reality." How others perceive me becomes my brand, with or without insight into the real me. And while most only see what's above the surface, it's our inner self, our core beliefs and values, our experiences, talents and strengths that make up who we really are.

So why is personal brand important? Our brand is what drives our decisions when no one is looking. Our personal and inner brand is what will come out naturally throughout the day as we make thousands of choices. Our brand is NOT our title at work or what appears on our business card. Our brand is much deeper. And one thing I tell all leaders, and I ask you to pause and think about this very seriously, is:

It's easier to get a good brand... than to lose a bad one.

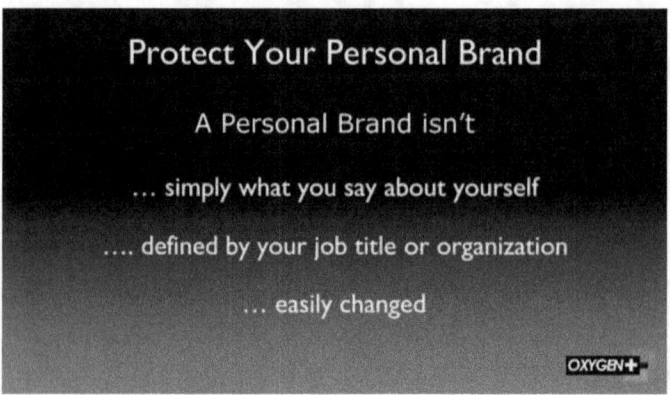

As an example, think about all of the good things you do on a daily basis. Think about those deeds as little drops of water. Think about all of the months and years you've deposited those drops of charity and acts of kindness into a bucket. Think about that bucket and how full it has gotten over the years. You've learned to dress and act with a certain persona that has become your schtick and gained you respect at work or in your community. After a few years, we don't even think about that bucket and how full it's become or what it looks like because it's become our identity. Everyone sees that your bucket is full and you're a relatively good, or maybe great, person (or company).

But, maybe your core beliefs start to weaken over time due to your environment. Maybe your bucket is so full that you believe you can take shortcuts when adversity strikes or money becomes tight and relaxing your standards becomes appealing. Maybe you get to a point where your core beliefs are compromised, and you make poor choices. Even worse, maybe the choice is so counter to anything you've done in the past, but now it's exposed to the world. Now, that full bucket of water has tipped over. It's empty. Your brand and all of the drops of good deeds, decisions, and choices over the years is EMPTY and on display.

Companies line the newspapers every day because of bad choices that instantly ruined once great reputations. Can these companies rebound? Sure, but not easily nor quickly. They, just like us, have to start refilling that bucket one drop at a time. It may take years for that bucket to be refilled, and it will take courage, perseverance, and humility. While I don't want to discourage anyone who has found their bucket empty, I do want to talk about having core beliefs and values that will guide you through the messy times (and there will be many) in an effort to make good decisions... even when no one is looking.

Warren Buffet said, "Lose money for the firm, and I will be understanding; lose a shred of reputation for the firm, and I will be ruthless."

When speaking, I always talk about the woman who taught

me about values and integrity, and I was lucky enough to have a front row seat to watch this lady make great choices... when no one was watching. That lady is my mother. A lady who is one of eight children, who grew up without the privileges we know today and still developed core beliefs about hard work, honesty, and giving more than getting. My mom owned two ladies clothing stores in a small Midwestern town for more than 50 years. It's not that the town could support two stores, it's the fact that people from 50 or more miles would drive to these stores because of "over the top" service and her ability to make them look and feel better about themselves when they walked out the doors.

But the story I like to tell most is that of a lady who was passing through our small little town for no reason (really, it's not a destination spot!). From what I understand, this lady was from Florida and, for whatever reason, decided to stop and shop along the way. She shared the same experience as so many others and found styles and a flair that you don't expect from small town stores. After making her purchase, she paid my mom and promptly left the store. As she drove off to wherever her destination was, my mom noticed that this lady had overpaid for her purchases.

Immediately, my mother went outside and walked up and down the street, to find her and make her aware. However, the lady from Florida had fled and was well along her way.

End of story? Not hardly! Fast forward over a year later. The chances of this lady coming through our small town again were minimal at best... except that she remembered the service and great styles she had found. She walked into the store and my mom immediately recognized her. Here's the part of the story that chokes me up when I'm speaking: my mom immediately walked over to her desk and pulled out an envelope. She then walked over to the lady and handed her the envelope, stating how sorry she was for overcharging her. Ladies and gentlemen, that's having core values and doing what's right... when no one is watching! Does it matter that the lady was probably surprised beyond belief, or that she had new found money and spent it (plus a lot more) that day... absolutely! But that was not my mom's intent. It was just to do the right thing! And had the women walked out without spending another dollar, that would have been okay, as well.

It's not about the result, it's about knowing that when you're consistent with your values in one area, it translates to every other area in your life. You can't be on your game just part of the time, it's you just being you every hour of every day, having a moral compass and values that guide your decisions when times are good... and when shaving corners seems tempting.

Developing your own core values is personal. It comes from the heart, deeply ingrained at a very young age, and doesn't change much. It's the bedrock of our behavior and the framework for making good decisions. I've mentored and coached young men and women who were looking for their moral compass. And while it's personal, it is also something that takes time and commitment.

I've attached a list below of which I usually ask clients to find what resonates within their soul and gives them energy. I encourage having no fewer than two but no more than five core values, as this number should assist you in making the right decisions throughout life. It's not that you can't change and modify it, it's just that over time you will realize these few words become who you are.

Once you've defined your core values, I would suggest journaling, and while digging within your soul, take each value and ask, "What does it look like to honor this value?" Write down specifically what situations it applies to and what life would look like when living this particular value without fail. Keep these thoughts close by and look at them constantly. Repeat your values daily and meditate and visualize what it looks like to live your values.

The Twelve Core Action Values
And the Cornerstones that Put Action into those Values

I. Laying a Solid Foundation
The first six Core Action Values and associated cornerstones develop inner strength of character.

II. Taking Effective Action
The second six Core Action Values and associated cornerstones catalyze action and contribution.

1. Authenticity	4. Courage	7. Purpose	10. Enthusiasm
Self Awareness	Confrontation	Aspiration	Attitude
Self Mastery	Transformation	Intentionality	Energy
Self Belief	Action	Selflessness	Curiosity
Self Truth	Connection	Balance	Humor
2. Integrity	5. Perseverance	8. Vision	11. Service
Honesty	Preparation	Attention	Helpfulness
Reliability	Perspective	Imagination	Charity
Humility	Toughness	Articulation	Compassion
Stewardship	Learning	Belief	Renewal
3. Awareness	6. Faith	9. Focus	12. Leadership
Mindfulness	Gratitude	Clarity	Expectations
Objectivity	Forgiveness	Concentration	Example
Empathy	Love	Speed	Encouragement
Reflection	Spirituality	Momentum	Celebration

I developed my core values almost out of necessity. Many years ago, my nephew, who had just graduated from high school, came to live with us, and suddenly, our house of three became four. Not that there were issues, but we found ourselves needing guidelines and a better way to challenge each other regarding the way we responded and the consequences (yes, this was just as much for me as everyone else). So we all sat down at the table, and I asked everyone to list their values and what resonated. After going through the exercise for a while, we whittled the list down to three simple values.

Faith

Respect

Responsibility

One of the reasons these values became so important was because it helped my wife and I avoid any sense of confrontation by simply being able to ask, "Is this consistent with your faith? Is this respectful to someone else or yourself? Are you being responsible?" Just asking these three questions covered so much ground.

We put these values on multiple sheets of paper and taped them to mirrors throughout the house. The ability to see and ingrain these values into our minds each morning, noon, and night helped each of us ask important questions and guide us through the day. And yes, I still use them by asking myself at the end of each day: 1) Were my decisions consistent with my faith; 2) Was I respectful to my wife, family, friends, and co-workers; and 3) Was I responsible? Did I do what I said I was going to do by honoring my faith, respecting others and delivering on my promises?

I'm sure the three you pick will be very different from mine; however, it's really about finding what can keep your bucket from spilling over as life comes at you from different directions. Whether it's at work or as a husband/wife, father/mother, or young adult trying to develop your moral compass, this is the method for building a brand and guiding you through each day.

Chapter 9 Key Concepts

- ☒ It's easier to get a good brand than to lose a bad one.
- ☒ Perception becomes reality... it may not be fair, but if enough people believe it, we need to recognize and adjust if necessary.
- ☒ Your brand is not the title on your business card or what you say about yourself... it's much deeper.

- ☒ Think of the "bucket example" when thinking about how quickly years of good decisions can turn into a bad brand.

- ☒ A bad brand can be changed, but it takes courage, perseverance, and humility.

- ☒ Developing your own core values is personal. It comes from the heart and is something you can count on to guide you through any decision.

CHAPTER 10

I'LL TAKE A GOOD ROUTINE OVER DISCIPLINE ANY DAY!

Any idea how many decisions we make each day? Take a guess... 500? 2,000? 10,000? How about 35,000 decisions each and every day... and sometimes we reach that limit by mid-afternoon. Just for context, a child makes approximately 3,000 decisions each day, (and with a nap) which is a reason why they have ABUNDANT energy in the evening when we're least equipped. From the time we wake up (excluding the fact that drinking coffee is a no-brainer), we have a multitude of decisions to make related to our hygiene, clothing selection, child drop-offs, travel to work (even if we work from home), pressing work related issues that someone felt the need to drop on you at 4:00 A.M... and that's before you even start working!

This chapter is one of my favorites! As leaders, we have to be efficient with our brains and the ability to process throughout the day. Once we've hit our quota (35,000) of decisions, we're officially defenseless. Our choices and thought patterns lose clarity. When faced with hunger, our desire to go off the rails is much easier. Our evenings turn into binge watching and demand little to no cerebral effort.

An excellent book written by Napoleon Hill in 1938, called *Outwitting the Devil*, puts Satan on trial with a truth serum so he can't lie. One of the key concepts of the book is that Satan loves a drifter. Someone who goes through life with no goals, intentions, or desire to get better. Basically, someone who has no routines and is perfectly comfortable... well... drifting through life. Hill calls such a state "hypnotic rhythm." Going through the motions with no plan to improve your relationships, health, career, or wellbeing is Satan's workshop. Developing good... no, GREAT routines, is critical for simplifying each day. Routines become habits, and habits simplify our lives by incorporating intentionality without expending energy for daily discipline.

When speaking of routines, I often speak of Steve Jobs. Have you ever wondered why one of the most influential minds in the 21st century wore khaki pants and a black t-shirt every day? One less decision to make! Steve Jobs was relentless when it came to routines and the ability to keep his mind fresh and vibrant throughout the day.

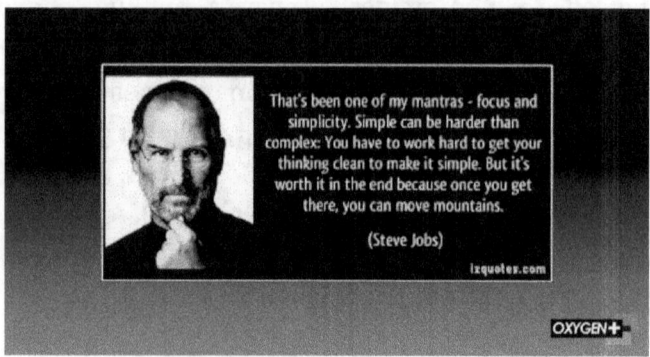

Steve Jobs references focus and simplicity (see Chapter 8 regarding essentialism). Simplifying your life and developing routines (think auto-pilot) with intention are critical to leadership. Two really good books regarding routines are *Atomic Habits* by James Clear and *The Power of Habit* by Charles Duhigg. Clear makes an interesting point in the beginning of *Atomic Habits* when he says to imagine a plane taking off from LA en route to New York. During the takeoff, the pilot decides to adjust the course three to five degrees south. No one on board will notice the difference. We're still headed in an easterly direction. However, over the course of the journey, when we deplane, we're stepping into the airport in Washington, DC. This slight and insignificant change in course over 3,000 miles landed us in a totally different location.

It's the same with any decision we make. Eating a pizza won't make you gain 20 pounds overnight, but over time, we all know the eventual outcome. This is why having clear routines and monitoring them weekly is essential to stay on course.

Routines are nothing more than a pattern of activities that gain consistency over time, and therefore, reduce the need for willpower and discipline. However, make no mistake, you can have the best routines on paper, but without the desire or system to take the first step, they become worthless. Having morning, pre/post work, and evening routines are essential. But how do we make routines consistent so we don't end up in Washington, DC?

Most experts (and found in the books mentioned above) refer to:

- Cue (a trigger or an act)
- Routine (the action)
- Reward (comfort/excitement)

This is really quite simple. Most of us drink coffee. We love coffee. We've drank coffee for years. It's become a habit. Our "cue" is to either fill the coffee pot the night before or just the desire for a jolt when we get out of bed. The "routine/action" is to hit the button, and well... we know the reward. The mental high and immediate energy from the java keeps us coming back for more each day.

The system was brilliantly used in the early 1900s, as noted in the book *Power of Habit* when a prominent businessman named Claude C. Hopkins was approached by a friend to launch a new product: a minty, frothy toothpaste named Pepsodent that he thought had great potential. At the time, Hopkins was one of the most famous advertising executives in the US, as exemplified by when he convinced Americans to drink Schlitz beer by boasting that the company cleaned their bottles "with live steam" while neglecting to mention that every other company used the same method.

However, in the early 1900s, almost no Americans brushed their teeth. And while Hopkins reluctantly signed on to take on the task, he needed to turn to a system he had used in all of his other successes: cue, action, reward.

"I made a million dollars on Pepsodent," Hopkins wrote a few years after the product appeared on the shelves, and he went on to say that the key was to "find a simple and obvious cue," and second was to "clearly define the rewards."

So how did Hopkins get Americans to start brushing their teeth? By taking advantage of a quirk in the neurology of habits. Even though it wouldn't be until almost a century later that medical schools and psychology labs would fully understand why habits exist and how they function, all Hopkins had to do was create a "cue," or a craving to make everyone believe that there was a need to brush. He sat down with a pile of dental textbooks; "It was dry reading," he later wrote in his autobiography, but he found a reference to the mucin plaques on teeth, which he later called "film." He then ran a series of campaigns having everyone run their tongues across their teeth, noticing a thin film that makes your teeth "off color" and invites decay. Even though film on teeth had existed since the beginning of time, the real culprit was sugar and other products that were eroding Americans' teeth at a staggering rate during the roaring 20s. But once he got everyone to start running their tongues across their teeth and feeling a thin layer of plaque, who wouldn't want a prettier, healthier smile by just buying a toothbrush and a new product called Peposdent?

Thus, Hopkin's had the final piece... The Reward. Three weeks after the first Pepsedent ad campaign, demand for the toothpaste exploded with so many orders that the company couldn't keep up. The product eventually went international and became one of the top sellers around the globe.

So how would you use the theory of cue/craving, habit, and reward? As for me, I started using it when I wanted to begin exercising each morning. To create the routine I had to set up a cue or craving. For me, the cue was putting my tennis shoes next to the bed and actually wearing my workout clothes to bed. This had to be done the night before to set the cue. In the morning, all I had to do was roll out of bed, and I had no excuse! Once I either made it down the hall to my in-home exercise equipment or drove to the gym, the habit was easier to execute.

And, I've already covered the reward in Chapter 5 when I wrote about the brain rush from exercising, including the lowering of cortisol (fear), the increase in serotonin (happiness), and dopamine (drive), and regulating the amygdala, which helps regulate focus, emotion, and the ability to handle the day ahead.

Is that all there is to creating habits? Not really. Although creating the cue/craving/trigger, the habit, and reward is widely used, we should also consider our environments. If you want to lose weight, I strongly suggest that you pack the pantry with healthy options. If you want to practice the guitar, I suggest you leave it in the room you use most. Just look at the people you hang around most. If you want good habits, surround yourself with others who apply good habits.

Another system mentioned by Clear is "intention." Having a clear plan of action and setting out specifics of when and where you'll carry out the habit you'd like to cultivate is essential. Having vague comments regarding "someday" or "after this happens, I'll…" is not a conviction. While I single out habits in this chapter, having the "energy" which comes from sleep, exercise, nutrition, meditation greatly increases your ability to develop, focus, and keep your routines sustainable by allowing you to rely less on willpower. In addition, having routines with a reward system that motivates "YOU" is essential. Even anticipating the euphoria of a positive experience (think Christmas day, feeling healthier, a much needed vacation) activates the neurotransmitters in the brain. So it stands to reason that the anticipation of the "reward" is a brain booster that gives us motivation to make a habit sustainable.

What about bad habits, such as mindlessly scrolling through social media, binge watching, alcohol, or other vices that we want to moderate or alleviate altogether. One suggestion is to identify something you value or fear (i.e., money, losing/competition, reputation). The ability to use these as motivators is very effective.

For example, if you want to lose weight and decide to track and list caloric intake each day, yet failing to do so would cost you $10 each day to a spouse, friend, or trainer, it stands to reason that the intensity meter will elevate quickly. Even non-monetary stimulus, such as "saving face," after telling everyone your desired goal/habit is a great motivator. In addition, the element of an accountability partner moves the success rate up measurably. Better yet is holding each other accountable where there is dual motivation.

A final suggestion is replacing one habit with another. One organization that uses this method to great effect is Alcoholics Anonymous. AA asks participants to list what exactly they crave from drinking. Usually, factors like relaxation and companionship are far more important than the actual intoxication. AA then provides new routines that address those cravings, such as going to meetings and talking to sponsors for companionship. The idea is to replace drinking with something less harmful. And while this is a very effective technique, AA also goes on to say that while this can work for a long period of time, stress and unexpected events can override this technique, leading one back to the old habit.

For this reason, I still point you and anyone wanting to develop sustainable habits back to the value of taking care of you (sleep, nutrition, exercise, positive relationships, mindfulness, and a deeper faith or purpose) as a way to keep your energy optimal and give you the best odds of creating successful habits.

How long does it take for a habit to become sustainable? According to a 2009 study published in the *European Journal of Social Psychology* by Phillippa Lally, it takes 18 to 254 days for a person to form a new habit. How's that for narrowing it down? Well, the article goes on to say that it ultimately depends on the habit in question, and additionally, some people adopt habits quicker than others because they are wired to want better or more rituals in their lives. Many people are familiar with the "21 days to form a habit" quote. This idea can be traced back to *Psycho-Cybernetics*, mentioned earlier in this book and authored by Dr. Maxwell Maltz in 1960. The problem, however, is that Maltz really never quoted this as a fact. He merely referenced this number as a "minimum number of days it takes to form a habit" by himself and his patients. However, the quote took on a new life as major "self-help" professionals, from Zig Ziglar to Brian Tracy to Tony Robbins, latched onto the metric. So while Lally's research used 18-254 days as a range to form a habit, the study went on to state that on average it takes more than two months before a new behavior becomes automatic (66 days to be exact).

However, as mentioned above, the new habit can vary based on the behavior itself, the person, and the circumstance. As a rule of thumb, consider it taking two to eight months to develop sustainable habits. And always consider that none of us are perfect. We can all fall behind on well-intentioned habits. It's the ability to stick with it, find the motivation, and develop the habit in an effort to reduce decisions and keep our energy optimal each day, for the rest of our lives.

What about the author's routines?

While my routines ebb and flow, breaking my routines into morning, pre/post work, and evening are most beneficial for me. My morning/evening routines are strongest, and my pre/post work routines are hardest to maintain.

Morning routine consists of:

1. As my eyes open, I start the morning with three to five rounds of "box" breathing to stimulate the heart and brain. Then a few minutes of prayer and gratitude followed up by positive visualization.

2. Make the bed. This is the quickest win I'll get all day. This sets the stage for success. It's my way of saying, "We got this... let's go!"

3. Eight to twelve ounces of lukewarm water with lemon (and a tablespoon of apple cider vinegar). After 12 hours of not drinking fluids, your body needs hydration (coffee is right behind). The water with lemon acts as a digestive and detoxifying agent in cleaning the liver, leading to better digestive health. For some, it can help with weight loss. In addition, this is a habit used by many world class athletes and runners.

4. Faith-based reading. You can choose what you like. For me, I want my morning consisting of Mind, Body and Soul. Getting my faith-based reading (15-30 minutes) prepares my mind and enriches my soul. For others, it might be anything positive, uplifting, and motivating. The key is to read. This is a habit I practice every morning.

5. Journaling. While I can't do everything listed and still start work on time, I do journal two to three days a week. In fact, for some, journaling before bedtime is a better way to fit the practice in and erase any clutter within.

6. Workout. I vary my workouts from stationary bike, tennis, weights/TRX bands, treadmill running, etc. However, this is also a key time for me to exercise the mind by listening to positive podcasts for stimulation and growth.

7. Meditation. I spend the last five to ten minutes of my workout "quieting the mind" and preparing for the day. I listen to both guided meditations and/or additional visualization.

8. Cold shower. Are you kidding me? Absolutely not. I finish a hot shower with water as cold as possible. I don't have time for an

ice bath or cold plunge, so a cold shower will have to do. The physiological benefits are wonderful. First, you feel invigorated (increased endorphins). Second, the cold water helps improve metabolism. We have two kinds of fat in our body: brown and white. White fat is what we associate with obesity and heart disease, but brown fat, which is elevated by cold temperatures, can regulate and lower white fat. Taking a cold shower at least two to three times per week may contribute to increased metabolism. In addition, cold showers have shown they can improve circulation, and fight off common illness. Because these are "quite invigorating," I suggest you start off with 20-30 seconds and condition yourself for much longer stretches.

By this time, my energy is peaking! As I've mentioned, you have to be a little "selfish to be a whole lot of selfless." A good morning routine is what separates the rich and intentional from the rest of the pack. And while you can read a lot about what time to start your day, the earlier the better. I've tried the 5 AM club but found my best sleep has me waking up at 5:45 and finishing my routine by 8:00. I realize everyone is in a different season of life and needs to modify what works. However, greatness starts in the morning. Even if your routine is only 30-45 minutes, the day ahead belongs to YOU!

Pre/Post Work Routines:

1. My pre-work routine is fairly simple. After hitting the on button for "command central," I bring up my bank account. I realized years ago that the longer I go without checking my bank account and credit card details, the more stress I take on. So my routine is nothing more than getting a daily dose of financial reality and keeping stress levels intact. For you, it may be another type of

stress. The key is to find what areas of your life cause anxiety and build daily routines to address them.

2. Now I'm ready to start my work day. And while this may not be considered a routine, the next step is to hit the "do not disturb" option on my laptop assuming I'm not in meetings. The first three hours of your work day are critical. This is the time to tackle the "big rocks." Remember, you just came off seven to eight hours of sleep and a great morning routine. Your "decision count" is as low as it will get for the day. Now is the time to work on the "big rocks" while you're at your best. These are the hardest, most high-level projects you have on your plate.

3. Post-work (evening) is nothing more than shutting down for the day and reviewing what's on my plate for tomorrow. Do I have my projects/tasks thought out, and what do I need to transfer from today's list? I find this routine harder at times as there is rarely "time to shut down." This has to be something you either do at the end of your day or as part of your late evening or morning ritual.

Evening routine:

I learned/borrowed my evening routine from Brendon Buchard, of High Performance Institute, and Ben Greenfield, of Ben Greenfield Fitness. It's called the 10-3-2-1 system, and I think it's great! It involves "dialing it down" in an effort to rest and activate your "parasympathetic nervous system."

> Our bodies have an autonomic nervous system. This regulates "automatic" or involuntary functions, such as breathing, sleep, digestion, sexual response, and many other cellular functions.
>
> The autonomic nervous system is divided into two subsystems: the sympathetic nervous system, which regulates fight-or-flight response, and the parasympathetic nervous system, which regulates the rest-and-digest response.

So while you think a few glasses of wine and a late night meal will help you fall asleep, it actually reactivates your nervous system, making for a restless night of sleep. The 10-3-2-1 system is:

1. Resist caffeine at least ten hours before bedtime.

2. Three hours before bedtime is a good time to quit eating. I mentioned in the nutrition section that I prefer to not drink wine nor eat food after 7:00 PM.

3. Two hours before bedtime is a good time to quit working. Hopefully you've quit before then; however, working while watching TV or multitasking doesn't give the neurons within our brains time to throttle down.

4. The final hour before bedtime is time to make sure all technology and LED screens are turned off. In fact, it's best to turn all the lights down low and allow the melatonin (the hormone that helps remind your body it's time for sleep) to kick in. This is a great time for me to read hard-back books, journal, and/or sit and talk with my wife. At worst, we watch something on TV, but it has to be light hearted (i.e., sitcom/documentary) allowing us to ease into a restful sleep.

Conclusion/Routines

Establishing routines and relying less on willpower and discipline are essential in all areas of your life. For example, the best golfers in the world have pre-shot routines, putting routines, pre/post playing routines, etc. Again, the value behind developing and instituting good habits is to live intentionally without having to think. It's the ability to use your 35,000 decisions on something other than mapping out each day from scratch. The key is to start small, write down your intentions/habits, and track them daily. It's a game changer, and I urge you to read the books suggested in this chapter and begin your journey to a GREAT day!

Chapter 10 Key Concepts

- ☒ We make over 35,000 decisions each day. We sometimes make these decisions by late afternoon, leaving willpower and discipline to guide the rest of the day.

- ☒ Bad habits can form without you knowing. Small, undetectable actions over time can lead to bad results/outcomes.

- ☒ Que, Action (the habit), and Reward are three critical steps for forming a habit. Que is the trigger to begin the habit, the habit is the action, and the reward is what makes the habit worthwhile and sustainable.

- ☒ Environment can influence good habits. Whether it be the friends you associate with or the food you keep in the pantry, your environment can lead to either good or bad habits.

- ☒ Essentialism is an effective way to simplify and keep daily decisions minimal.

- ☒ To create good habits, be clear and concise. Start small if you need to, but be consistent and incorporate an accountability partner to help keep you on track.

- ☒ It takes between two and eight months to form a habit. There are many variables depending on the habit itself and the individual.

CONCLUSION: THE OBSTACLE IS THE WAY

The Hardest Chapter to Write

I had a boss one time that said something that I found humorous but didn't realize how relevant it would be later in life. He said, "Stan, at some point we have to believe our own bullshit." While he was right, I never knew how important that phrase would be until I began consulting and coaching and relying on what I've read, sometimes however, without first-hand experience.

Throughout this book, I've espoused fifteen years of research, reading, coaching, and personal insight. And while I try to live the principles researched in this book, experience is the best teacher. Absent of experience, you need to believe your own bullshit. For that reason, I find the best coaches are those who have lived a life of hands-on experience and been in the foxhole.

Currently, I'm coaching a great guy whom I met several years ago, and who has set up a not-for-profit organization aimed at helping prisoners get a soft, Christian-based landing after serving their time, in an effort to offset recidivism. The reason he'll make a great coach is because he's lived "that life." He was released from prison in 2004, with many demons in hand. He knows the feeling of re-entering society and the challenges on the other side. As I told him, they can't BS you because you know what they're thinking before they do. While I wouldn't wish his experiences on anyone, living the life he's lived has prepared him to be the best coach and advisor imaginable.

Over the past several years, my wife and I have gravitated towards Phoenix with the thought of possibly living there in the future. Our daughter and son-in-law moved to Scottsdale years ago, so it made sense to spend more time in Phoenix and take advantage of all that it has to offer. One of those advantages is having a great health care system in Scottsdale, with Mayo having both a clinic and hospital. Because we wanted the best health care possible, we chose Mayo as a place to have our annual physicals given the experiences we had with them many years earlier in Rochester, Minnesota. Currently, we split our time living in Florida and Iowa (you should be able to pick which seasons we live in which location based on the fact that we love warm weather). And although that made getting our physicals in Scottsdale a little more challenging logistically, it also provides another reason to spend time with our daughter and son-in-law.

However, the fall of 2018 was different. We weren't sure how, but we just knew it was different. My wife started having a few more medical issues; however, the doctors in Iowa ruled out anything severe but did notice inflamed lymph nodes. So as time moved on, we knew the next round of physicals in October might not be as smooth as what we had experienced in the past, and soon thereafter, we made our trek to Scottsdale.

Watching the one you love go in for a test is one of the hardest things in life to experience. I can vividly remember when the test results were completed, and she met with her doctor for the results. I was asked to sit in the waiting room and tried to rest my mind by taking business calls. However, at the end of my call, knowing that I would be in the room with her in a few minutes, I absolutely broke down... without even knowing the results. I could sense this time was different.

As they called me back to the doctor's office, my wife, whom I've known since third grade, met me in the hallway to say, "I have cancer." Specifically, she had Non-Hodgkin's lymphoma— of which I had no idea what that meant. We met with the doctor, and she handled the conversation beautifully as she braced us for the road ahead. The doctor ended the conversation by saying she could beat this type of cancer and the odds are getting better. My wife was more accurately diagnosed a week later with stage four cancer, and it had spread to her bone marrow. However, at the time, the fact that she could recover was all that I was hanging on to. There was a journey in front of us... and we had to embrace it.

In the book, *The Obstacle is the Way* by Ryan Holiday, he quotes the stoic Marcus Aurelius, who penned his thoughts and beliefs regarding life's challenges, and stated sometimes these challenges allow us to grow and see unintended results we never imagined.

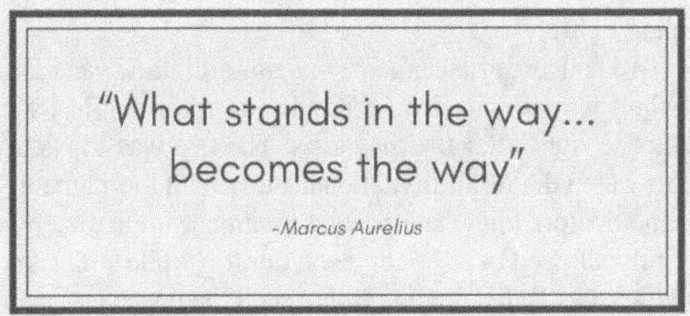

Knowing that my wife and I now had an unplanned obstacle and journey ahead, the obstacle now reminded me of what my boss had said several years ago, "At some point... we have to believe our own bullshit." As the journey became crystal clear, the need to "double down" on every paradigm in this book was inevitable. Whether we had first-hand experience or not, every principle we believed or experienced now became very real.

First of all, as arrogant as it may sound, I had to take care of me... because I absolutely had to have the energy to give every ounce of my energy to my wife. And make no mistake, this isn't about me, but it's about what I believe, researched, and embraced through the years that led up to this time of uncertainty.

In Chapter 1, I discussed my friend Jerry, whose cancer is in remission, and that his recovery centered around many of the principles mentioned in this book. Keeping stress out of the lymph nodes (which interestingly, is the type of cancer my wife has) is directly related to her physical, emotional, mental, and most importantly, her spiritual well-being. And as I reached out to Jerry during this time, I was immediately reminded of the quote that he so eloquently said after telling us of his cancer:

"When Death Becomes Certain, Life Becomes Rich."

While we still had multiple treatments to consider and a long journey ahead, this resonated ten times over because life was becoming rich!

We had already planned a once-in-a-lifetime vacation earlier in the year with our daughter and son-in-law that just so happened to be right after the diagnosis. The trip was to Maui and Oahu to watch the Maui Invitational Basketball tournament. And while the doctors knew she needed treatment immediately, they reluctantly allowed us to continue on our trip while still acknowledging the risk. Balancing the future with the present was numbing to say the least.

The afternoon that we landed in Maui, she received a call from her doctor to set up the appointment to have a portal put in for receiving chemotherapy, radiation, and immunotherapy upon return. They told her of the hair loss, to which only she could find a silver lining: thinking of the great hats to buy on the trip. Yet, we all carried on as only a family could. We put the future on the back burner and experienced everything Hawaii had to offer in the present. This was our first time seeing these beautiful islands, and actually the timing couldn't have been better.

The second call from my wife's doctors happened to take place while whale watching on a boat. And again, only in a response you can expect from her, she peacefully said, "I couldn't think of a better place to talk to an oncologist." We hiked, shopped, and ate, and in usual Gibson/Schultz fashion, worked the day flawlessly from sunrise to sunset. This was our way of experiencing "when death becomes certain, life becomes rich."

A year and a half has passed... and my wife is cancer free! Yes, it can return, and she'll go through two years of continued treatments, but LIFE IS RICH! Many lessons were learned during this process and with a little grace from God as well! When we returned from our vacation in Hawaii, my wife was given an option of "trying" immunotherapy first, without the chemotherapy and radiation. While this is still in the experimental stage, it has been effective in some cases but not all and may have a higher chance of returning. The "cocktail" (all three drugs) puts a severe strain on the body, so she elected to try immunotherapy alone with the hope that it will work for several years as medicine continues to advance. She's absolutely blessed—as they not only nailed the treatment, but she has had absolutely no side effects along the way. We give so much credit to modern medicine and God's guiding hand, and we learned to "believe our own BS" and see the amazing effects physical, emotional, mental, and spiritual living has on our lives, and how they were enriched along "The Way."

My wife recently shared one of the lessons with me that I hadn't picked up on. When asked what was going through her mind after the diagnosis, she quickly responded, "It was not knowing the plan nor the steps ahead that was the hardest part."

Her anxiety and fears lessened as the doctors revealed the plan, schedule, and potential outcomes. It's a state we all live in at different points in our life. The lack of a plan, a direction, and intentionality is paralyzing and creates fear. However, whether working it out on your own, or with a mentor/coach, the clarity and intentionality creates a sense of peace and direction.

A second observation was the healing power of relationships. We truly believe the speed of her recovery, especially the remarkable results, after just the first three months was due to the richness of time spent with our daughter and her husband. As mentioned in Chapter 6, positive relationships and experiences reduce inflammation and open the arteries to the heart (which is what Non-Hodgkin's lymphoma attacks). We believe dialed-in prayers and an outpouring of love from family and friends was essential to the healing process.

And as mentioned, this was a time to "double down" on

everything this book has to offer. From optimal sleep, nutrition, exercise, loving relationships, prayer, meditation, and routines, we believe these practices along with amazing doctors and medicine provided the "ultimate cocktail." While it's an experience you wish for no one, I personally never felt more dialed-in in my entire life.

My intent for this book is about "YOU" taking care of "YOU," so you can take care of "OTHERS." This is the life that Jerry was talking to me about. This was 15 years of research regarding living a rich and intentional life with an opportunity to test my own BS. And while my heart breaks as we know so many die each year from countless diseases, this story is more about how to live with richness and intentionality on your way to reaching your God-given design. It's about the fact that while everyone dies, only a few live! Those who live well have rich routines, relationships, and experiences. It's about making a decision right now... this very minute. It's knowing when you are sick and tired of being sick and tired! When will you say enough?

The path ahead may be costly as you engage coaches and mentors, read a multitude of books, listen to podcasts, journal, and feverishly find your "why." But climbing on board to a rich and intentional life is the right choice. I've put several books and references in the appendix as a starter kit.

I mentioned in the forward a comment made by a young executive after one of my presentations when she said, "I never thought my life could be changed in one hour." But her life wasn't changed in that one hour, it's being changed day-by-day in the days ahead with her willingness to take a new journey. It's her belief that there's more to life and she has the courage to reach for it. It's her decision to live each and every day and striving to be all that God intended her to be... it's her new quest to find "The Way" through living a rich and intentional life.

May you all Live a Rich and Intentional Life!

AFTERWORD

You can tell from this book that I not only enjoy new paradigms but also bio, life, and productivity hacks. I like to know the physiological, biological, and neuro effects these techniques offer, which often give me greater insight into why I should practice them. And trust me, I recognize that while I have a strong understanding of the paradigms written, there are other industry experts, like Ben Greenfield, Tony Robbins, Robin Sharma, Michael Hyatt, and countless more who have boundless expertise. I urge you to check out their messages and add them to your reading/podcasts list.

My uniqueness is that I cover a little more ground than most. I've lived and breathed inside both the corporate and entrepreneur life for more than 35 years. I know and understand the politics and real life challenges as an employee and leader.

In addition, as a leader and personal development coach, I've added additional areas of expertise to now include career consulting and finances. While I'm not a financial advisor, I, like many of you, need better routines, goals, and a mind-set to relieve the anxiety associated with revenue generation and controlling expenses.

In addition, I've researched and employed productivity hacks for better focus and goal driven results along with multiple options for digital and analog daily planners.

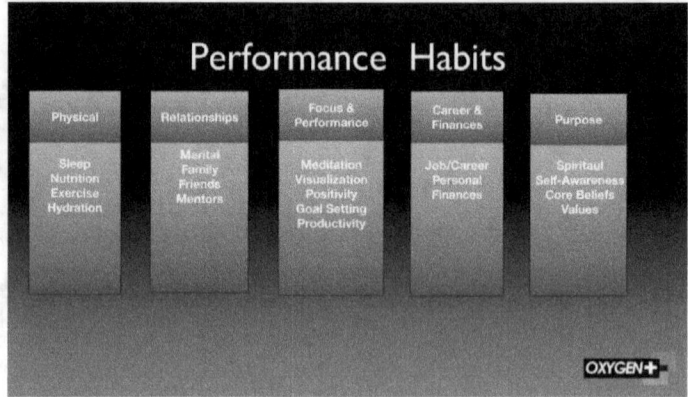

As mentioned, my desired legacy is to transform and lead over 100,000 lives to personal greatness. I'm passionate about helping leaders and companies grow exponentially! I'm finding more and more opportunities working with Gen Z and Millennial entrepreneurs. I'm so impressed with their fearlessness and knowledge of business and also with their maturity to acknowledge the "gray hair" experiences of those older. And leadership starts at the top. I prefer not to work with companies in which the leader only wants his or her direct reports fixed. As Gallup, Inc., an analytics and advisory company, so wisely said, "Employees don't quit companies... they quit leaders." The best leaders I've known are full of humility and have a thirst for making others great!

Thank you for reading or at least glancing through my first attempt as an author. I realize you've been fed with a firehose of information and let me be the first to tell you that while I've tried and followed most paradigms discussed, life often gets in the way. I don't lead a legalistic lifestyle and I suffer from the same ice cream, pizza, and sugar cravings as you. While the leadership and personal development techniques in this book can probably be found in most self-help books, my uniqueness is that I've been in your shoes as a spouse trying to get better, a father juggling a career and wanting more, an employee getting beaten down at times, and a friend who fails to reach out as often as I should.

I'm writing this book during the COVID-19 pandemic. I've latched on to the phrase "don't let a good pandemic go to waste." If this pandemic has shown me anything, it's that I can accomplish so much without the pre-COVID distractions that eschewed valuable energy. I find my clients are all looking for purpose and meaning. I'm learning that goals and dreams are necessary, but the journey is what's really special. The ups and downs, the trial and error, the good times and challenges are what makes our life unique.

This book isn't about wholesale changes, but finding a few new nuggets that make today and tomorrow a little better. Over time, allow yourself to expand and begin a journey of being special. Being "YOU" and no one else. You are unique and no one else can take your gifts away unless you let them. Choose to be better... Choose to be special... Choose YOU so that you can develop the energy to make OTHERS better.

There's no better time to write a new story. Go and live a Rich and Intentional life... You've got this!

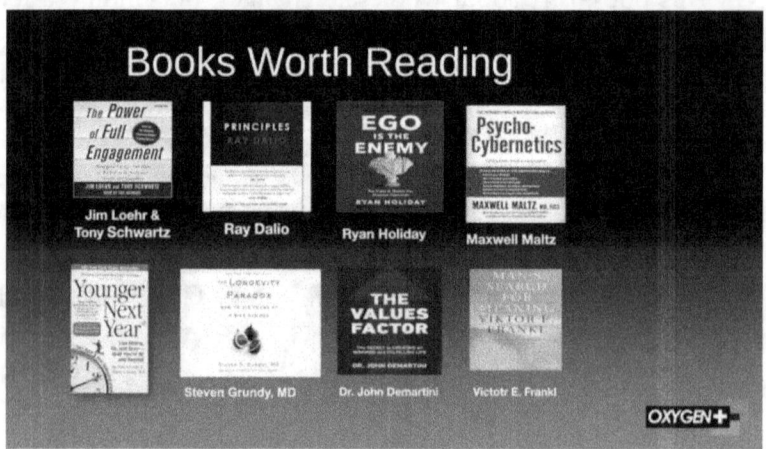

ACKNOWLEDGEMENTS

This book has been a journey and passion for way too long. I sincerely thank so many family and friends for making (I mean, encouraging) me to write and take my practice to the next level. Thanks babe (my wife, Sharon) for being what everyone in the world calls you: "Saint Sharon." Thanks to my daughter, Kadi (and her husband Eric), who I've always called my moral compass (shouldn't it be the other way around?). Thanks mom for always telling me to lead when I was young and making me believe I actually could. To my sis, Nancy (and my brother from another mother Mike), for believing in me and creating wonderful opportunities for me to spread my message! Thanks to all of my friends and colleagues for making my life rich in so many ways. And thanks to all the clients, whom I call leaders, for teaching me more than I taught you... and thanks to the Father, Son, and Holy Spirit for blessing me with those mentioned above, and those I'll be blessed to meet going forward.

ABOUT THE AUTHOR

Stan Gibson has over 35 years of experience as both a corporate and entrepreneurial leader. He has become a sought after speaker throughout the US for his message that both engages and inspires others to greatness. In addition to being a leader in small, medium, and large cap companies, he also coaches and consults with high growth leaders and businesses in all industries. Stan's extensive research in leadership development is now in print as *Living a Rich and Intentional Life* is now available on Amazon Books. Stan has his Masters in Corporate Real Estate (MCR) and has been a lecturer, panelist and instructor on various real estate topics for more than 20 years. In addition, he has his coaching and mentor certificate from Grandview University, and he serves his passion to transform and lead over 100,000 leaders to personal greatness. Stan can be reached at www.oxygen-plus.net and welcomes anyone wanting to lead a rich and intentional life!

www.ingramcontent.com/pod-product-compliance
Lightning Source LLC
Chambersburg PA
CBHW070636220526
45466CB00001B/195